Celebrating
JUSTICE &
LIBERATION

CELEBRATING SERIES
edited by Linda McKiernan-Allen

Celebrating Incarnation: A Resource for Worship

Celebrating Covenant: A Resource for Worship

Celebrating Justice and Liberation: A Resource for Worship

Celebrating
JUSTICE &
LIBERATION

A RESOURCE FOR WORSHIP

Linda McKiernan-Allen, EDITOR

CHALICE
PRESS
ST. LOUIS, MISSOURI

Scripture quotations, unless otherwise noted, are from the *New Revised Standard Version Bible*, copyright 1989, Division of Christian Education of the National Council of the Churches of Christ in the United States of America. Used by permission. All rights reserved.

Scripture quotations marked (NIV) are taken from the HOLY BIBLE, NEW INTERNATIONAL VERSION®. NIV®. Copyright © 1973, 1978, 1984 by International Bible Society. Used by permission of Zondervan Publishing House. All rights reserved.

Scripture quotations marked (Jerusalem) are excerpts from *The Jerusalem Bible*, copyright 1966 by Darton, Longman & Todd, Ltd., and Doubleday, a division of Bantam Doubleday Dell Publishing Group, Inc. Used by permission.

Cover art: Stained-glass window, Bethel Lutheran Church, Herman, Minnesota; photograph © The Crosiers
Cover and interior design: Elizabeth Wright
Art direction: Elizabeth Wright

This book is printed on acid-free, recycled paper.

Visit Chalice Press on the World Wide Web at
www.chalicepress.com

10 9 8 7 6 5 4 3 2 1   03 04 05 06 07 08

Library of Congress Cataloging–in–Publication Data
Celebrating justice and liberation: a resource for worship/
Linda McKiernan-Allen, editor.
    p.   cm.
    ISBN 0-8272-0487-6 (alk. paper)
    1. Justice—Biblical teaching. 2. Worship programs. I.
McKiernan-Allen, Linda.
    BS680.J8 C45 2003
    264—dc21

                                                    2002154027

Printed in the United States of America

Contents

Preface

Within the worship life of Christendom, language of "justice" emerges in scripture, prayer, hymn, and at the table. Underlying the most basic of relationships within the Christian faith, "justice" speaks of the ways that God would have us treat one another so that all people may live, may live fully, and may live together.

This volume of worship resources provides materials to be used in connection with fifteen different texts: five texts from the Old Testament and ten from the New Testament. Each speaks of some particular aspect of justice or of a particular moment within the faith community's life of awareness concerning God's justice.

Each text serves as the well from which prayers and meditations are drawn to form one chapter. Each chapter provides a call to worship, an opening prayer, a prayer of confession, words of assurance, prayers of the people, a children's sermon, two sermon starters, an offering meditation, an offering prayer, a communion meditation, and a benediction. The book also provides a chart suggesting hymns and anthems keyed to each of the fifteen texts.

One possibility would be to use these texts and resources to focus on the over-arching theme of justice for a series of services. They can also stand alone, or pieces from a service might be used within a service without using every piece.

Contributors

Marian Y. Adell, United Methodist minister, Ph.D. from Drew University in Madison, N.J., currently serves as pastor of Community United Methodist Church, Dayton, Ohio.

Erik Alsgaard, ordained in the United Methodist Church, is Assistant General Secretary for Communication at the General Board of Church and Society of the United Methodist Church, based in Washington, D.C.

Judith Ann Brown, an ordained deacon in the United Methodist Church, is serving as minister of music at University Park Christian Church (Disciples of Christ), in Indianapolis. Her B.S. (in music education from Lebanon Valley College in Annville, Pa.) and Masters in Sacred Music (from Union Theological Seminary, New York City) undergird her ministry. Judy and her husband, Bill, have two adult sons, Hoyt and Doug. Judy delights in finding an exceptional connection between hymns and scriptures.

Nancy Dickinson engages life as a retired United Church of Christ pastor and educator, following ministries in both United Church of Christ and Christian Church (Disciples of Christ) congregations in Indiana.

Judy Fackenthal pastors Garfield Park Baptist Church in Indianapolis and is a graduate of Christian Theological Seminary in Indianapolis.

Rob Fennell is ordained as a minister in the United Church of Canada and serves at Islington United Church in Toronto. He enjoys good liturgy and multiple styles of worship, and is always glad to help design worship that leads us closer to the heart of God.

Bill Humphreys serves as chaplain for Carroll College in Waukesha, Wisconsin. Ordained in the Presbyterian Church (USA), Bill is father of three and husband of one.

David Kinsey has been a Quaker pastor for more than seven years. He continues in the historic concern of Friends for the dignity and equality of all people. He and his wife, Rosie, are the proud parents of four beautiful children.

Harvey and May Sweet Lord. Harvey Lord, minister, emeritus, of University Church, Chicago, and May Sweet Lord, retired teacher from Chicago Public Schools, are presently volunteer coordinators of Disciples Justice Action Network. They continue a lifelong commitment to strengthen the link between Christian faith and justice action.

Laura Loving is a United Church of Christ minister serving the Heritage Presbyterian Church in Muskego, Wisconsin. Co-author of *Celebrating at Home: Prayers and Liturgies for Families,* Laura is interested in creating worship resources for a variety of settings. She is a retreat leader, writer, pastor, substitute teacher, mom, and spouse. She also writes curriculum and enjoys the integration of educational ministry and worship. Both are venues for following the mandate to seek justice, love kindness, and walk humbly with God.

Liza Lynnette Miranda Santiago (Master of Arts in church music from Christian Theological Seminary in Indianapolis and Bachelor of Music in vocal performance from Chapman University in Orange, California) was born in Bayamon, Puerto Rico, in 1973. Currently she serves as music minister in the Iglesia Cristiana (Discípulos de Cristo) in Jardines de Caparra, Bayamon, Puerto Rico.

Susan Shank Mix is a freelance human being, retreat leader, liturgical dancer, elder, teacher, butterfly, mother, grandmother, lover of life and celebrator of rainbows, a pilgrim on the journey that is home. She is an associate member of an ecumenical partnership church of the United Church of Christ and the Christian Church (Disciples of Christ) in Squaw Valley, California, and a member of the board of the Council on Christian Unity for the Christian Church (Disciples of Christ).

Amy G. Moore is worship coordinator for First Christian Church (Disciples of Christ) in Lynchburg, Virginia. She enjoys planning worship and using resources such as litanies, prayers, and hymns that draw the congregation into worship and truly make the liturgy "the work of the people" as the scriptures are brought to life for our lives today.

David Phillips is married to Debbie, has one son, Michael, and has two wonderful grandchildren. He has pastored the Wabash (Indiana) Friends Church for more than twenty-five years. He always looks for ideas and ways to more effectively communicate the good news found in the Bible.

Rebecca Button Prichard pastors Tustin Presbyterian Church in Tustin, California. She has also served parishes in Scotland, Indiana, and California. She received her Ph.D. in theology from the Graduate Theological Union in Berkeley, California. She authored *Sensing the Spirit,* published by Chalice Press.

Frederick W. Smith, Minneapolis, Minnesota, is an active member of Lake Harriet Christian Church and the Metropolitan Interfaith Coalition for Affordable Housing (MICAH). Why justice work? "Because according to Micah, it's one of the few requirements of the faith; besides, Mother said I should."

Lucy Rupe Watt presently serves the Presbyterian Church as executive presbyter of Winnebago Presbytery. She lives out "doing justice" by volunteering as a mediator with the county court system. Lucy enjoys traveling, reading, and making new friends. She is the grandmother of a brilliant two-year-old granddaughter.

Edward C. (Ted) Zaragoza, Presbyterian minister, Ph.D. from Drew University, currently serves as Associate Professor at United Theological Seminary, Dayton, Ohio.

Genesis 18:1–15

Laura Loving

CALL TO WORSHIP

Leader: The Lord appeared to Abraham by the oaks of Mamre.

People: God is full of surprises!

Leader: Abraham jumped up to offer refreshment and rest to the travelers.

People: May we be ready to respond to God's presence!

Leader: Sarah and Abraham hosted their visitors with urgency and generosity.

Women and Girls: May our hearts be open to the One who nourishes us with the Word and feeds us at this table.

Men and Boys: May our lives be open to the least and the lost whom God loves.

People: May our table be open to all who hunger for justice.

Leader: God had dreams and hopes for Sarah and Abraham.

Men and Boys: May we be hospitable to God's hopes and dreams for us.

Women and Girls: Come, let us worship the One who is both Guest and Host, both Nourishment and Nurturer, both Dreamer and Hope itself.

People: Let us worship God with the urgency of our praise and the generosity of our song and silence.

1

OPENING PRAYER (UNISON)

God of surprises and sudden interruptions, break
through our routine and our ritual and stir us
here. Whisper to us to move beyond what we
expect. Sing to us to risk more than we imagined.
Urge us to give more than we thought we had.
Help us to hear your voice in the voices of those
in need—
in need of nurture or nourishment,
in need of shelter or spiritual guidance,
in need of wholeness or healing.
Help us to listen for you in this time of worship.
Move us with music.
Make us wise with your Word.
Silence our chatter through prayer.
Lift us beyond ourselves to meet you at the
intersection of holiness and laughter.
There, at the welcome table, feed us and make us
whole with the presence of Jesus Christ. We pray
in Christ's name and for the sake of the world.
Amen.

PRAYER OF CONFESSION

O God, you know us better than we know ourselves.
You know what we are capable of doing and how we have
fallen short. You know how wide mercy can be and how
narrow our hearts have been. So bear with us as we pray
aloud the ways we have sinned. Wait for us on the other
side of prayer and wrap us in your forgiveness.

*(Leader pauses as people first read silently through the list/
litany. People then join voices with the leader on those things
with which they particularly identify. The leader's voice
carries through the entire list.)*

We have not loved our neighbor as ourselves.
We have blamed the poor for being poor and have
overlooked our own spiritual poverty.

We have closed the doors of our church to those in need.
We have lost our sense of wonder and our faith that
with you, all things are possible.
We have failed to welcome the crack of an egg yolk
dawn.
We have ignored the diamond necklaces of
constellations overhead.
We have laughed at the possibility of bringing to life
your promises.
We have lived in luxury while others barely live.
We have turned our backs on your call to be lovers of
justice and peace.

(Silent prayer)

Have mercy on us. Enfold us with forgiveness as we
turn toward transformation in Jesus Christ. Amen.

WORDS OF ASSURANCE

God's mercy is from everlasting to everlasting.
There's a wideness in God's mercy.
It's a love that is so wide it covers all our sins.
There's a wideness in God's mercy.
It's a love that is so deep it reaches the profound
wounds of our hearts.
There's a wideness in God's mercy.
It's a love that is so old it spun out the planets,
spoke through the birth of Isaac,
led through the lives of Abraham and Sarah,
called forth the prophets,
blessed and bled in Jesus Christ,
and still sings through the ages.
**God's mercy and love are from everlasting to
everlasting.**
There's a wideness in God's mercy.
Let it transform you and me. Amen.

IN RESPONSE, SING "THERE'S A WIDENESS IN GOD'S MERCY."

PRAYERS OF THE PEOPLE

O God, we give you thanks for the stories of people of faith—the stories that wrap themselves around us and will not let us go. We praise you for your mystery and the methods of your divine madness that created life in Sarah, a woman well beyond the childbearing years. We are in awe of your choices of human beings, faithful but flawed, to give birth to your vision of hope for the world. For Abraham's humanity, for Sarah's laughter, for the narrative that winds its way into our lives, we give you thanks.

We are mindful, O God, of the ways this story brings pain. Bless those who live with the questions of infertility, whose laughter has turned to mourning, who look for you but cannot find you, who live in fear or anger or depression or exile.

Bring comfort to them.

Host them at this table and bind up their wounds.

Send us searching for them in the streets and alleys and suburban cul-de-sacs and church pews. Help us to see them in our mirrors. Make us instruments of your healing, midwives of justice, bearers of peace. We pray in the name of Jesus Christ: the Great Story, the living narrative, the holy laughter in our souls. Amen.

CHILDREN'S SERMON

This can be rapped, chanted, or told rhythmically with clapping or stomping interwoven through the storytelling. Find ways you can involve the children in this process and choose the style with which you are most comfortable. Soli deo gloria.

> I'm gonna tell you a story 'bout Sarah.
> A woman way up in her years.
> Now this Sarah had no children,
> which had often brought her to tears.
> So God came to visit ol' Sarah
> and her aged husband Abe.
> And told them, "In due season,
> this woman's gonna have a babe."

And Sarah laughed, laughed, laughed.
And she did laugh.
Now Isaac is a name that means laughter,
and that's what she named her son,
so that everyone ever after
could tell the story of this special one.
Our God is full of surprises.
Maybe even for you and me.
So children, open up your eyes
and see what you can see.
Will God find a way to work through you?
Could you be a bringer of peace?
Is God giving you something to do
that will give the captives release?
Oh, big words tell this story.
But it's simple as it can be.
Just open your lives to God's glory.
There are surprises for you and me.
So let us laugh, laugh, laugh.
Let us laugh!

SERMON STARTER: HOSPITALITY UNDER THE OAKS OF MAMRE

The hospitality Abraham offered to the visitors under the oaks of Mamre was typical of the Near Eastern custom at the time. It challenges us to think about our hesitation to be hospitable in our day. Surely the pitfalls of being taken advantage of, of risking safety or comfort, or of inconvenience (our common excuses for our lack of hospitality) were a part of the human experience in biblical times as well. But the norms were very different, and Abraham's actions would be considered faithful and appropriate.

There are even several stories from other ancient Near Eastern cultures as well as the Greco-Roman world about gods coming to visit, sometimes three at a time, to announce the birth of a child.

You might work with hospitality in its archetypal forms and contrast it with the fear-full "gated communities" that our churches have become. Conversely, you might point to continuing traditions of hospitality, as in Catholic Worker houses, homeless shelters, Benedictine retreat centers, cooperative community projects, and even new-member inclusions and greeting habits of congregations.

Look at the verbs *ran, bowed, hastened,* and the adverb *quickly*—all this in the noonday heat in the desert. Is this a model for our discipleship or our discipline of hospitality? Commentators do not make a causal connection between this urgent response and the birth announcement, nor do we want to practice our faith "so that" God will bless us. The reverse causality might be stressed: We practice our faith "because" we know the goodness of God, not "so that" God will give us great news. Be careful of making direct correlations, being mindful of the anguish of unfulfilled dreams, infertility, loss, and unanswered prayer represented in the congregation. Point to the Lord's table as a place of healing and hospitality for all us travelers.

Other treatments of hospitality might include our openness to God as an act of hospitality or our willingness to invite the "other" into our midst (cross-cultural pollination, barrier-breaking, generational understanding, the theology of immigration policies, etc.).

Finally, you might deal with the traveler image as one that we all can identify with—and think about modern parallels for offering refreshment to one another in Christ's name. Notable resources include Delia Halverson, *The Gift of Hospitality: In Church, In the Home, In All of Life* (St. Louis: Chalice Press, 1999); John Koenig, *New Testament Hospitality: Partnership with Strangers as Promise and Mission* (Minneapolis: Fortress Press, 1985); Ana Maria Pineda, "Hospitality," in *Practicing Our Faith,* ed. Dorothy Bass (San Francisco: Jossey-Bass, 1997); and Christine Pohl, *Making Room: Recovering Hospitality as Christian Tradition* (Grand Rapids, Mich.: Eerdmans, 1999).

SERMON STARTER: DOING THE MATH

Sarah and Abraham have one complicated marriage. Their past arrangements of complicity, compromise, and conflict have set the stage for this dramatic story of bearing the child of promise. Spend some time setting up the history of this couple and their people. Some feel that this story is inserted into the tradition to explain the genesis of Isaac's name. But even more, it is one of the texts that illustrate ways that God restores the divine promise just when the moment of peril is about to descend. God restores the promise of Genesis 12:1–3.

Much is made of Sarah's laughter; little is made of her denial. Her response is one of many biblical texts in which people respond in amazement to amazing announcements, such as the Shunammite woman's response to a man of God in 2 Kings 4:16 and Mary's response to an angel in Luke 1:34. You could use Sarah as a model of receptivity, surprised by joy, and create a sermon around this idea.

Some feminist theologians assert that Sarah is a pawn in the patriarchal game.

Alice Ogden Bellis reviews some of the feminist interpretations in *Helpmates, Harlots and Heroes* (Louisville: Westminster/John Knox Press, 1994). She describes Esther Fuchs' interpretation of culturally clued storytelling in this way:

> "Biblical mothers, including Sarah, are depicted in ways that advance the patriarchy, in particular the man's desire to control women's sexuality and reproductive capacity. Throughout the Abraham-Sarah sequences, Fuchs believes that Sarah is marginalized. She appears only in contexts where her sexuality or reproductive ability comes into play, and even then her role is limited. This is particularly evident in the annunciation scene, in which she is literally sequestered in the tent, where she can only overhear the birth announcement" (73).

But Bellis allows that while still a victim of patriarchy, Sarah may represent an advance over ancient Asian and African counterparts. Savina Teubal suggests that Sarah's lack of children is not barrenness but her role as a priestess. (See her book *Sarah the Priestess: The First Matriarch of Genesis* [Athens, Ohio: Swallow Press, 1984].)

There are several different reconstructions of Sarah's story, which may bear fruit as you explore the broader question of representation of women in the Hebrew Scriptures or Sarah's role in the history of our faith family or identity formation as based in scriptural model. The possibilities abound for the courageous preacher!

A simpler approach might include a play on the math metaphor: Sarah had little to laugh about, on the one hand, given the strange parade of charades she and Abraham had been in. On the other hand, what joy, what delight, what irony! She was doing the math in her head. She knew she was too old, but she also knew that God was a proponent of "new math" even back in those days. Numbers, age, and mathematics were not the issue. Naming the issue from Sarah's womb was at the heart of the promise—coming through with the promise of progeny and a place in the history of God's people.

You do the math. Explore the mystery of God's actions in the midst of human foibles.

Here, three visitors = one Lord: $1+1=3$ as Isaac comes into the picture. Descendants are multiplied. This is not a linear, logical story, but the kind of math I prefer—one in which God keeps "showing the work" in new formulae and delightful variations on the old rules.

So it is fitting to celebrate this story as you move to the "multiplication table" to break bread together. This is the place where God's grace is enough for all, where abundance wipes out scarcity, where all our math about who can be fed and who should be free is canceled out in the broken bread and the cup poured out.

This is One; we are many; it is enough. (You may want to use the hymn "One Bread, One Body".)

Master the new math of God's economy of justice. It will make you laugh for joy. For at this table, we recall that with God all things are possible, even with frail human beings as bearers of the promise. We are fed at this table, and the bread is multiplied, and the cup keeps pouring, and we have no other way to respond but to laugh out loud with a "Yes!" and to run, wheel, crawl, walk, or dance from this place into our places of work and play and rest and relationship, and practice the new math of God.

OFFERING MEDITATION

Our hearts are like Sarah's womb: surprised by joy, laughing at the lavishness of God's promise, open to the preposterousness of God's gifts, bearing forth the fruits of our labor. Let us offer our gifts to God.

OFFERING PRAYER

Most Holy One, in faith we offer the issue of our
    hearts.
Use these gifts to promote peace and to spread the
    good news of your love.
Use us in our neighborhoods,
in our work and in our play,
in our ministry and in our mission,
to bring about your reign of justice. Amen.

COMMUNION MEDITATION

When the Lord came in the guise of travelers to the tent of Abraham and Sarah, the response was predictable. Mandated by custom and faith, the hosts quickly prepared a meal of cakes and calves and cooling drink.

As we come to this table, we have prepared the meal in a predictable way, mandated by custom and faith. The bread is here. The cup is here. And the Lord is here too: feeding us with presence, filling us with hope. The Lord is also here in the guise of travelers at this table: the young and old, the newcomer, the stranger, the charter member, the newly baptized—the Lord is present in each of these. Look around and see the face of God in those near you. Close your eyes and see the image of Christ in those who long to be fed, who yearn to be free, who hunt for homes or jobs or health care. Open your hearts to sense the urging of God's spirit.

This is the Lord's table. May you find grace and courage here. Amen.

BENEDICTION

People of the promise,
go from this place, brimming with generosity,

fed by hope, expectant with the seed of justice,
great-with-possibility.
May God bless you as you live generously out of the
    promise,
  as you share hope with others,
  as you nurse and nurture and nudge forth the deeds of
    justice,
  as you grow great as a community—
  feeding the hungry, housing the homeless,
  hearing the cries of the suffering, learning from the
    poor,
accepting the impossible surprises of God's presence.
We go in peace, to love and serve God. Amen.

Exodus 5:1–2, 4b–12, 15–18; 5:20—6:1

Frederick W. Smith

CALL TO WORSHIP

The earth is the Lord's!
And all her peoples.
All power is the Lord's.
And justice is in God's hands!
Come, let us worship together!
Let us give God our thanks and praise!

OPENING PRAYER

Ever-living God who calls us to live in peace, we gather here in your name. Come and melt the tensions of this world, that we may realize your presence here. Mold and fire us with your word, that we may again be your new world. Ever-loving God, make your presence known to us, we pray. Amen.

PRAYER OF CONFESSION

Leader: God of the prophets, your word is like no other.
Men: You challenge our complacency.
Women: You call us to commitment.
Men: Yet we prefer relying on ourselves.
Women: We have chosen our own excuses in place of your love.

Leader: God of Moses and Miriam, of David and Ruth, of
          Isaiah and Amos, of Elizabeth and Mary, forgive us.
Women: Forgive our calls for self-reliance and turn us to
          rely on you.
Men: Forgive our self-serving ideas of what is right and
          open us to your vision of love and justice.
Women and Men: Forgive our willingness to settle for
          words, and hold us to your call for action.
All: **Merciful and loving God, forgive us.**

WORDS OF ASSURANCE

Hear this assurance from Isaiah:

If you offer your food to the hungry
and satisfy the needs of the afflicted,
then your light shall rise in the darkness
and your gloom be like the noonday.
The LORD will guide you continually,
and satisfy your needs in parched places...
and you shall be like a watered garden,
like a spring of water,
whose waters never fail.

(Isa. 58:10–11)

PRAYERS OF THE PEOPLE

O great and awesome God, you have thrown the stars
across the sky and set the sun on its course; you have raised
the mountains and filled the seas. You have scattered the fish
throughout the waters and filled the air with birds. You have
created your human family in all sorts and conditions of
people.
Ever merciful and ever loving God, hear us, we pray.
For all the children, especially those whose lives are
          already shattered by neglect, hunger, homelessness,
May we welcome them into our family of care.
For all the young people, especially those whose hopes
          and dreams are constrained by poverty, the bands
          of racism, or the bonds of self-doubt,
May we welcome them into our family of care.
For all adults who are challenged with illness without

health care, the burdens of work without adequate
compensation or representation, for immigrants in
a new land or those who are strangers in their own
land,
May we welcome them into our family of care.
For those who are old and near the end of this life,
especially those who are lonely, who are afraid,
who must rely on others for their room and
board,
May we welcome them into our family of care.
For all of us, O God, in need of your love, in search of
your truth, trying to do our best and wanting to do
better,
Welcome us, O God, into your family of care.
In Jesus' name we pray.
Amen.

CHILDREN'S SERMON

In our Bible lesson today, Moses learns a very important
lesson about doing the right thing.

I want to ask you a question, and you need to think real
hard about your answer.

When have you tried to do your best to do the right thing
and it's only gotten you into trouble?

For example, have you tried to play with your little
brother or sister, and you've tried to give them toys, you've
sung to them, you've done everything you know to do, and
they still keep crying?

(Do the children have examples?)

Have you tried to cook breakfast for your mom or dad
and had it end up a great big mess in the kitchen with nothing
good to eat?

Have you tried to help someone in your class at school
and gotten into trouble with the teacher for talking?

(Again, do the children have things to say or examples?)

Have you ever gone to return a toy that you really like
that you've borrowed from your friend (who really likes it
too), and then on the way to your friend's house you trip
and fall and break the toy?

All these are something like our Bible story today. Moses did all he could to help his people. But what he did only got the people into more trouble with Pharaoh. It was right at that point, when Moses had done everything he could, that Moses needed (and was given) God's help. When we can't do any more, when we've tried our best, we have the promise that God will help us.

Let's pray. Dear God, thank you for the story of Moses and what it teaches us.

Help us to remember that when we've tried our best, we have your promise of help.

Thank you. Amen!

Sermon Starter Background

Chapter 5 of Exodus is often misread to mean that Pharaoh required the Israelites to make bricks without straw. Not so. What Pharaoh required was that the Israelites gather the straw themselves rather than the Egyptians providing it for them. This scattered the Israelites "throughout the land" to gather the stubble or straw and, thereby, greatly increased the time it took to make bricks.

Sermon Starter

Exodus 5 is one of the few chapters in the Exodus narrative in which God is not an actor. God's name is invoked by Moses and Pharaoh, but the actors in the chapter are all entirely human. God does not enter the narrative again until Exodus 6:1. Moses and Aaron's roles are central in causing Pharaoh to come down even harder on the Israelites. The first reaction of the Israelite supervisors is that there must have been some mistake, and they go back to Pharaoh evidently in the hope that he will change the order. Rather than looking to God, the people look to Pharaoh. Only when Pharaoh again calls the people lazy do they realize that their hope in Pharaoh is misplaced; then they turn in anger on Moses and Aaron. Moses is trying to do his best but only gets the people into more trouble. Moses then, also in anger or at least in confusion, turns to God. And as if in response to Moses' anger, God in 6:1 steps in and says, "Now you will see my plan."

SERMON STARTER

Even though God is not directly mentioned in the chapter, it is evident that God is using Moses to "harden Pharaoh's heart." In a very real sense, God finishes what Moses starts. In coming down harder on the Israelite slaves, Pharaoh gives two reasons for his actions. First, the people are "too many," and second, they are "lazy." (The parallels to present-day criticism of the poor and of welfare are obvious.) The story graphically illustrates how difficult social change is. Things must get harder before they get better; that is, the people have to give up their hope in Pharaoh's doing the right thing and have to come to rely on Moses and God before they are willing to leave the familiar routines of even slavery and enter into a new way of life. Work for justice often leads to a worsening situation when the current political leadership is challenged to do the right thing; ironically, this becomes God's way of bringing the people to the point that they are willing to follow Moses and God. It's also evident that Moses doesn't know what God is up to. Moses asks for a three-day feast in honor of God. There is no mention of freedom for the people. Did Moses think they could journey into the wilderness to sacrifice to God and then sneak away? More likely, Moses had no idea of exactly how the people would be freed. So, too, with justice work. Campaigns begin with a goal in mind, but how to get there is never clear, because the political situation keeps changing. What we can do is to keep the vision, the goal, the dream clear.

OFFERING MEDITATION

We worship God, who through Moses led the Israelites out of slavery in Egypt to the freedom of their own land. We worship the God of prophets and of Jesus, who described God's beloved community where the meek inherit the earth and where love and justice prevail.

This history and vision are certainly cause for celebration. But they are also calls to action. Calls to participate in God's work of liberation. We begin this work with our offering.

Moses learned that liberation would come not through his efforts but at the end of his own efforts, when he offered himself as an instrument for God's work of freedom. And so, like Moses, in response to God's word, we offer our money and ourselves for God's work toward the freedom of justice.

Offering Prayer

O God, accept these offerings of our money, our skills, our time. We know the work of our hands is not enough, so we offer our hands for your work. Accept us, use us, O God, for your work, for your justice, for your peace. Amen.

Communion Meditation

The exodus story is certainly not the only one of God's helping the poor. The Bible is full of accounts of God helping the poor, the stranger, the outcast. Our God has what some have called a preference for the poor. Perhaps because the calls for help that come from the poor remind us that we are brothers and sisters, members of the same family. Perhaps because the homeless of our city streets testify to the continuing need for love and justice. Perhaps…

One thing, though, is clear. As our forebears so clearly emphasized, all are invited to the table of the Lord. All are invited to the celebration of God's love. Here no one is turned away for lack of individual responsibility or other judgments of character; there are no time limits on the love that is offered. There is only the unconditional invitation to all those who believe.

Come, eat, and drink. Let us celebrate. Together with all of God's great family, let us come to the table of justice and peace.

Benediction

O God of power, send us forth,
That our lips, which have sung your praise, may now speak your truth to power,
That our hearts, which have felt your love, may now be open to all your family,
That our hands, which have shared your bread and wine,
may be your hands for justice and peace, now and forever. Amen.

2 Kings 4:1–37

Amy G. Moore and Susan Shank Mix

CALL TO WORSHIP

The spirit of our God is upon me,
because God has anointed me:
to bring good news to the oppressed,
to bind up the brokenhearted,
to proclaim liberty to the captives,
and release to the prisoners…
to provide for those who mourn in Zion—
to give them a garland instead of ashes,
the oil of gladness instead of mourning,
the mantle of praise instead of a faint spirit.
I will greatly rejoice in the LORD,
my whole being shall exult in my God!

(from Isa. 61:1, 3, and 10)

OPENING PRAYER

God, we know we do not need to invoke your presence,
for you are already with us. You are with us in joy and in
grief. You hold us when we are anxious and concerned. You
love us even when we are argumentative and frustrated. You
forgive us when we sin, and you dance with us when we are
happy. You are present where there is injustice and when
justice is finally accomplished.

You were present here before we walked in this morning. May your creative, dancing, loving, forgiving Spirit celebrate with us as we worship you. In the name of the One who showed us what "God-with-us" looks like we pray. Amen.

Prayer of Confession

Dear God, this morning we confess we have not acted in just and loving ways in your world and for your people. We have heard the cries of our neighbors and not answered them. We've been aware of injustice in our own lives and taken no initiative to solve the problem. We've offered bandages and bread when the world needs healing and jobs.

Forgive us for our lack of initiative and caring. Stir in us the passion and the power to work for peace and justice in your world. Open our eyes to see injustice, our mouths to speak on behalf of justice, and our hearts to persevere in the ways of justice in the name of our brother, Jesus. Amen.

Words of Assurance

God has created us to live in peace with one another. We are loved and we are forgiven. Praise be to God! Alleluia!

Prayers of the People

We do not celebrate justice in a vacuum. We read the headlines, listen to the news, live in our own neighborhoods and communities, and sit next to our friends in the pews. We know that justice is still needed in many places and by many of God's people.

During this time of prayer please name aloud a person, a situation, a cause of which you are aware. After each statement please say, "This is the world in which we live." The congregation will then reply, "Hope be in us and in the world." I will offer a closing prayer.

Wait for prayer statements or requests. Gently remind the person to end with "This is the world in which we live" [or say it for them]. After each statement, lead the congregation in responding, "Hope be in us and in the world."

At the conclusion of the requests, pray:

God, who fills our empty life-vessels with the oil of hope, we give you thanks for all the ways in which justice is expressed in the world. We call upon your gifts of grace and power in the situations voiced this morning. Hear, too, the unspoken prayers of our hearts. Make us continually aware of injustice whenever and wherever we find it. Help us to know deep in our souls that with your help we can move toward a world of peace with justice, even as we recognize that this is the world in which we live.

Hope be in us and in the world.

This is the world in which we live.

Hope be in us and in the world.

CHILDREN'S SERMON: KEEPING PROMISES

Give highlights of a "stone soup" story (such as *Bone Button Borscht* by Aubrey Davis [Toronto: Kids Can Press, 1997]). Tell the scripture story of the woman and the oil (2 Kings 4:1–7), perhaps from the perspective of the children in the story. Talk about the role the neighbors played in the story. Do you think it was a big deal for each neighbor to give the widow a jar or two? How do you think they felt when they heard that she was able to sell the oil and pay off her debt?

> Prayer: Dear God, please help us know how to love our neighbors. Give us open hearts to share. Remind us that together we can make a difference in the world. Amen.

SERMON STARTER BACKGROUND

Genesis 17 occurs in the context of despair, anguish, and growing disbelief that God's promise of children to Abram and Sarai will ever be fulfilled. They had left their home; journeyed to Canaan; survived famine, deceit, and battle; and accumulated great wealth and land, but still had no child from their marriage by the time they were 99 and 90, respectively. The text struggles with "the powerful claim of the promise and the equally powerful reality of being without an heir" (Walter Brueggemann, *Genesis*, Interpretation

[Atlanta: John Knox Press, 1982], 153). The covenant between the parents of our faith and God calls on Abraham and Sarah to believe "in a gift from God which none of the present data can substantiate" (152). In this passage, Abraham disparages God's promise as impossible to fulfill, then tries to circumvent God's time line by asking to substitute Ishmael for the son he doesn't believe he will ever have with Sarah. Finally, Abraham reaffirms his commitment to the covenant with God by circumcising all the males in his household, and continues to await the fulfillment of the promise.

Sermon Starter: 2 Kings 4:1–7

Think about how oil was used in biblical times. It was used in cooking as it is today. It was used as fuel for light. Oil was used as medicine (externally and internally), bringing physical health. It was used in consecrating priests, who were to bring spiritual nourishment to the soul.

Given all these life-giving uses for oil, is it any wonder that its presence was a symbol of gladness and prosperity, while its absence indicated sorrow or humiliation?

When Elisha asks, "How can I help you? Tell me, what do you have in your house?" the widow still had a little oil. She was holding on to that which was useful, which could nourish body and soul. But she was very close to humiliation. She stood before Elisha with an urgent request for help: A creditor was about to take her two children away as slaves, and as a widow, she had no resources except a little oil.

This oil was the most valuable commodity she had. But she also had another resource: her community. "Ask your neighbors for jars," says Elisha, "and not just a few." The community became a necessary part of the solution for the widow and her sons. It gave her the means, the vessels for a miracle.

What courage and faith it must have taken for her to move beyond her comfort zone and ask for help, believing that by doing this, her situation would be relieved.

The jars gathered, she follows Elisha's instructions. She goes into her house with her children, and she shuts the door. Perhaps she leans against the door and breathes a prayer:

"Oh dear God, what have I done? What happens now?" God is present in that holy moment as she begins to pour the oil into the jars. God's grace pouring the oil of gladness, of comfort, of prosperity, of justice, into jar after jar. And when the last jar was full, the oil stopped flowing. We don't know why there were no more jars—whether she stopped asking, or if those were truly all the jars of the community. We do know, however, that if there had been more, the oil would have continued to flow, for our God is one of abundance. As Jesus said, "Give, and it will be given to you. A good measure, pressed down, shaken together and running over, will be poured into your lap. For with the measure you use, it will be measured to you" (Lk. 6:38, NIV).

Yes, justice is accomplished through faith, along with hard work. (When the jars were full, the woman still had to carry them to market, sell them, and manage her finances.)

The injustice of the widow's situation was resolved, beginning with a resource she had, using tools from her community, and demanding faith and hard work. The good was accomplished through God's power and grace.

"How can I help you? Tell me, what do you have in your house?" On a spiritual level, God may be asking us, "What gifts do you have to offer in this situation?" In the midst of economic injustice, instead of just throwing money at a need, we must ask, "What resources are here already?" From our own experiences we know that when we invest ourselves in solving a problem, the outcome is more satisfying (for example, "sweat equity" of new owners in a Habitat for Humanity house). Justice-seeking doesn't come about as a personal, solitary venture. The whole community needs to be drawn into finding a solution. When that happens, the benefits begin to add up. And when God's grace and power and love enter the equation—multiplication!

How does this happen? Consider 2 Corinthians 4:7. We have the treasure of God's love and grace through Jesus Christ in the clay jars of our bodies. God chooses us as God's vessels for miracles, multiplying in us gifts of grace and caring and bringing justice through us to the world.

Sermon Starter: 2 Kings 4:8–37

The following is written to be preached. If, however, you have a dancer in your congregation, you might ask her, him, or them, to interpret the emotions and movements in the first part of the sermon as you share them verbally.

Imagine yourself in a wonderful, open space ready to watch an amazing dancer in concert. As you wait, you read the program notes. Ray Stedman has written these:

God has given gifts. Paul calls them "graces," and we have different gifts, according to the specific gift of grace that is given to us. I like that term for gifts because it indicates something about them. Graces are graceful. Something that is graceful is a delight to watch, and this is true about a spiritual gift. A gift is an ability God has given you because he wants you to do this thing so naturally, smoothly, and beautifully that others will take note of it and ask you to do it and enjoy watching you do it. You will enjoy it, too. When you are using your spiritual gift you are fulfilled. It is called a "grace" because it is not a difficult, painful thing to do; it is something you delight in doing. And you can improve in it as you do it. Therefore it is one of the things that will make life interesting and fulfilling for you.[1]

"Graces are graceful. Something that is graceful is a delight to watch." The lights go down, and into our vision comes the Shunammite woman, who is graceful, grace-filled, and a delight to watch.

In the first act of the dance she is filled with hospitality and offers it generously to Elisha. She opens her home, enlarges it, and prepares a welcome space in which Elisha may eat, study, and live. We see a nurturing, welcoming God reflected in the movements of her dance.

---

[1]Ray C. Stedman, *From Guilt to Glory*, vol. 2, *Reveling in God's Salvation* (Portland, Oreg.: Multnomah Press, 1978), 113. Quoted by Marva J. Dawn, *Truly the Community* (Grand Rapids, Mich.: William Eerdmans, 1992), 96.

God surprises us, as the dance increases in energy when Elisha is inspired to offer her something in return. The hidden strength and power of the dancer is revealed as she responds firmly both to the offer of government help and to the offer of a child. In one case she is not interested. In the other, she refuses to be teased or tormented by a hope that cannot be fulfilled. Intimate, loving, comforting God shines forth, however, when she does become pregnant.

The second act opens. The child has grown old enough to accompany his father to the fields. All is well. Then the child is stricken with a headache, taken to his mother, and dies in her arms. See our suffering God reflected in the mother's movements as she grieves the death of her son. God, present and comforting, stirs the woman to action on behalf of herself and her child.

Laying the child on his bed, she gathers the few things she needs for her journey and leaves, telling her husband, in faith, "Everything is all right." The strength of her dance is evident as she approaches Elisha. Through him, she yells at our listening God (to whom we can come in the worst times of our lives.) She is relentless in her faith. Elisha can do something. Her faith and power urge Elisha to action beyond what he believes himself capable of doing. The easy way, the "bandage," does not work. Simply laying something on the problem does not solve it. Elisha must become involved. At that point, God's power moves through Elisha. The child is restored to life and to his mother's arms.

The point of the dance analogy? We are all given the grace-gift of God to work for justice in some way, shape, or form. We often hear about the "struggle for justice," the "long road to justice," and the "march for justice." That language and the reality often tire us out just thinking about them, much less committing ourselves to doing anything about justice. Justice is hard work. Yes, it is. The dancer who leaps "effortlessly" from the stage floor, pauses in midair, and lands, only to leap again, has stretched and trained for strength for hours, days, or years to prepare the muscles for those leaps.

But God has given each of us gifts for justice. Some of us march; some of us build; some write letters; some testify before city councils and school boards; some of us travel beyond borders; some of us dance; some preach; some go to jail as either prisoner or advocate. When we are following our calling, fulfilling our special gift, the struggle is less, the road is shorter, and the march is more like a parade. Let us celebrate together the grace-gifts for justice that God has given us. Whatever our calling, our gift, within it is the power to work for justice with grace and beauty. We will be filled with joy, and our dance of justice will be seen to be grace-full.

OFFERING MEDITATION

Like the widow, we are called to give all that we have to the cause of justice. We are called to work hard and be creative. Like the Shunammite woman, we are called to take the initiative and be persistent in the cause of justice. As we offer our gifts, let us give thanks to God for the miracles of money, hard work, and persistence that happen every day so that the people of the world might know justice.

OFFERING PRAYER

God who has filled our beings with gladness and generosity, take these gifts we bring and multiply them in the world as you multiplied the oil so many years ago. Use them to bring your justice, your peace, your love into a world so desperately in need of healing. Use us as instruments of your power. We pray in the name of Jesus, whose Spirit continues to teach us to walk the way of peace with justice in the world. Amen.

COMMUNION MEDITATION

Read aloud 2 Corinthians 4:7–11 from the NRSV.

Just as the miracle of the oil and the recovery of the child witness to the extraordinary power of God, so does the miracle of bread and wine at this table. Through this meal we carry the death of Jesus in our bodies so that his life of peace and love and justice might be made visible in the world through us. Eat this meal with gusto. Do not be stingy in the taking of the bread. Do not be reticent in the sipping of the wine. You are taking the power of God into yourself. Do so with energy and deep, abiding compassion for the world of God's making and the people of God's love. Through the power of this meal you can be made different, and you can make a difference.

BENEDICTION

> You came to this place because you believe in the
>   power of God to make a difference.
> Go from here filled with the energy of the Holy Spirit.
> Be persistent in your cry for justice.
> In the name of Jesus the Christ, move the world a little.

Jeremiah 18:1–11

Rob Fennell

CALL TO WORSHIP

Come, friends and seekers of God, come and worship.
**This is the right time; this is the right place; we are
the right people.**
Come and worship God, three-in-one; come to be
nurtured and shaped by the One whose love and
care for us is deeper and wider than we can
imagine.
**We open ourselves now to experience God's presence,
to delight in song and prayer and word, so that we
may be molded in Christ's image.**
Come, friends and seekers of God, come and worship.

OPENING PRAYER

Loving God, in whose plan of grace we are as clay, take
us once again in your hands in this time of worship. Shape
us inwardly, mold us, throw and remake us, until our ready
spirits have been filled once again. Create us as vessels able
to hold the treasures of your word and carry them forward
into the world you love. In the name of Jesus we pray. Amen.

PRAYER OF CONFESSION

It is true, God of the ages, that even as we try to do our
best, we often forget to open ourselves to your leading. We

act as though our plans and agendas might single-handedly change the world. Forgive us, Lord God, for the wrong we do and the good we leave undone. Soften our hearts when they become hard; reshape our minds when they become rigid; water our spirits when they become dry and cracked. Remake us in your image, O God of second chances, so that our lives, our words, and our actions may show forth the glory and wonder of your love. Forgive us, gracious Christ, and help us to follow you with renewed energy and vision. Amen.

WORDS OF ASSURANCE

God's love is wider than the horizon. God's grace is deeper than the sea. God's mercy is higher than the mountains. God's forgiveness reaches out to you and me. For all who repent and seek a new life in Christ, God's love, grace, mercy, and forgiveness abound. Friends, receive the good news of the gospel.

PRAYERS OF THE PEOPLE

Loving God, we come to you once again, grateful that your ear is always open to our stumbling prayers. We pray in the Spirit, who prays for us and with us. We pray in the name of Jesus, who came to you each day with an open heart. Lord God, we offer our praise for all you have done, for the goodness of your plans.

Help us to see the ways you move in our lives and in our world. Lead us to a deep gratitude, colored by generosity with what you have given us.

We praise you for the wonders of life: the vulnerability of a baby, the brightness of a child's eyes, the strength of a teenager's determination, the wisdom of later years. We rejoice in the delicate smell of pine, the sweet taste of honey, the joyful sound of a friend's laughter, and the gentle touch of someone who loves us. You are good to us, God, and we thank you.

Hear our prayers for our world. We pray for peace in the dozens of conflicts around the globe, especially _____ and _____. We pray for wisdom and justice to fill the minds of all who lead the nations. We pray for dedicated persons who go abroad to offer relief and assistance. We lift up our prayers for our nation, as we long for communities that are safe and filled with light. We pray for compassionate leadership that sees human needs and opportunities, not just impersonal market forces.

Hear our prayers for this our church community, as we seek together to know you and love you well. Reach into each of our hearts today, we pray; shape us and mold us so that our words and actions may bring glory to you and advance the purposes of your realm. May our church be a place of safety and hope for all who come through our doors.

Hear also our prayers for ourselves, gracious God. You know us well. You know our deepest needs and fears and joys, which we lift up to you now in the silence. *(Pause for a few seconds.)*

Praise and thanks be to you, Holy God, maker and lover of all creation. May all that we are bring you joy and gladden your heart, for we love you, and we are yours. Amen.

CHILDREN'S SERMON

If possible, bring in real clay and a potter's wheel, or use modeling clay. You might invite a potter to come and demonstrate, either in worship or following your worship time. If you don't have access to workable clay, bring some clay objects (pitcher, cup, bowl, etc.) and make do with play dough or homemade modeling clay. Work with the clay in your hands as you talk through the story and images that the Jeremiah text suggests.

Tell the story from Jeremiah 18.

Say that God shapes us and leads us so that we may be of service. Show how different shapes can be used for different purposes *(create a quick bowl, an oil lamp, and/or a cup)*. Talk about what objects you brought and what their purposes could be. Suggest how different children might have different purposes (bringing joy, pointing to God's presence in the world, helping others).

A closing prayer could ask God to shape us, as a potter shapes the clay, so we may know who we are, know the gift that we are, and enjoy the good work God gives us to do. At the end of the children's time offer each person a piece of the clay. *(Alternatively, a piece could be given out to each at the start of the story time.)*

SERMON STARTER

There is a hard word of judgment at the end of this passage (v. 11). What rings true about this, as we tremble before the God of righteousness? Where does our sin flourish? This will be difficult (and perhaps unpopular) to preach about. But it remains true that not everything we do as individuals, communities, and nations pleases God—love is not blind, in this case. Without pointing fingers, be aware of your own sin (which is likely to be similar to others')—your own tendency to leave God out of your plans, to turn away when discipleship gets too hard, or to exclude or hurt others even as you try to defend yourself. What are the social/systemic sins of our day? Entrenched racism, the greediness of market economies, consumerism, and conspicuous consumption come to mind. What else does your evening paper or newscast reveal?

Now where is the gospel? The good news resides in the restless unwillingness of God to leave us in a state of alienation from God and God's purposes. God persists in sending prophets, in opening hearts to the Word, in pouring the Spirit into those who believe, in offering us grace in the sacraments, all so that we are not left to our own devices. Jesus himself was and is all about bringing us close to God. God's spirit seeks to bridge whatever gap exists and renew us for creative, loving, openhearted, and openhanded service.

The prophecy of Jeremiah 18:1–11 is a warning, as is most Old Testament prophecy: Get it together and come humbly to God, who makes and breaks history, because sin is real. Our repentant hearts open the door to God's grace flooding in to set things right again.

Sermon Starter

Rather than emphasizing the note of judgment, approach the text attentive to the opportunity it offers. God does not merely make the world and then leave us to our own devices (contrary to popular belief). God remains passionately invested in the way things flow: Witness the intervention of prophets old and new, and of Jesus Christ. If God cares so deeply for us and for all creation, what shape do our responses to grace take?

The basics of Christian spirituality are one place to start: worship, prayer, Bible reading, and service. (Too often we have stressed one or two of these and neglected the others.) Within this quad-pattern are many opportunities to connect with God, receive God's grace, and respond with thankfulness. What opportunities does your congregation offer? Be specific. What might your faith family do to expand those possibilities so that everyone has a way to grow within the quad-pattern? Be visionary. Encourage your hearers to take up the challenge to be fully devoted followers of Jesus. Challenge your hearers to imagine what might come next in your life together. Provoke a hearing of the text that leads your hearers into new visions of what could be as we try together to build the just, sustainable, loving, free, mutually supportive, and transparently honest community in which everyone wants to live. On that journey toward communal wholeness, God is a wise guide, seeing what is needful and shaping us like clay by the Spirit.

Offering Meditation

What has God put in your hand? Just as the children could see different objects emerging from the clay, what gifts are emerging in your life? What gifts of time, talent, and treasure might you share in the coming of God's realm of justice and joy? God loves a cheerful giver, so let us give from the heart.

Offering Prayer

Gracious God, who with wisdom and care shapes all creation for the purposes you have planned, we offer these gifts, and ourselves, with gratitude and celebration. Use them and lead us so that they and we may be fit vessels for the coming of your reign of justice and joy. Amen.

COMMUNION MEDITATION

This table is spread in anticipation of the heavenly banquet that awaits us. The saints and friends of God have gone before us. Now in the Spirit of God, we may join them and the living Christ, who is our host. Come not because you must, but because you may. You are invited to share in the goodness God has prepared. Come and remember; come to be commissioned to the life into which God is calling you. These are the gifts of God for the people of God. Come, for all things are now ready.

BENEDICTION

Upon you may blessings flow. Into your heart may suppleness of Spirit come. Within your mind may the mighty potter, God, work the clay of your life, shaping and recasting until your will and Christ's are made one. Go with the peace of God, who made you and loves you and calls you God's own creation. Amen.

Micah 4:1–6

Erik Alsgaard

Call to Worship

Lord, open our lips.
And we shall declare your praise.
Teach us to walk in your ways;
Teach us, O God, to walk in your paths.
This is the day that the Lord has made.
Let us rejoice and be glad in it!
—or—
A journey of many miles begins with a single step.
Guide us and support us in our journey, O God.
I was happy when they said to me, "Let us go up to the house of the Lord!"
Come, let us go up to the mountain of the Lord, that God may teach us God's ways.
God's ways are not our ways; God's ways are not of our making.
God's ways are peace, love, and joy, removing fear from our lives.
God has called us to God's Holy Mountain, to learn the ways of peace, love, and joy.
Thanks be to God!

Opening Prayer

Almighty God, whose house has been established as the highest, where people come from around the world to learn of your ways: Grant that we who gather here today may learn of your ways of peace, that we shall not learn war anymore nor teach our children war anymore, through Christ our Lord. Amen.

PRAYER OF CONFESSION

O Lord God, we thank you for the gift of your Son, Jesus Christ, the Prince of Peace. With him you have given to us prophets and disciples, teaching us the ways of peace in your realm. We confess to you, O Lord, that we have not always followed the ways of peace. We have offended others and you. We have often followed the easy path to hatred instead of the hard path of love, forgiveness, and mercy. We have said unpleasant things to your children. We have sold our souls for quick profit and easy lives. By the actions of your Holy Spirit, O God, fan the embers of our hearts that we may be afire again for your love, peace, and forgiveness. Grant that we may go forth from this place bathed in your love, to bring peace, hope, and joy to a hurting and hopeless world. Amen.

WORDS OF ASSURANCE

This is the message we have heard from [God] and proclaim to you, that God is light and in [God] there is no darkness at all...If we walk in the light, as [God] is in the light, we have fellowship with one another, and the blood of Jesus [the Son] cleanses us from all sin. (1 Jn. 1:5, 7)

PRAYERS OF THE PEOPLE

Almighty and most gracious God, we give you thanks and praise for this day and for again calling us to worship in this, your house. We give you thanks, also, for the teachings you have given us:

The stories of Adam and Eve, Jacob and Joseph, Abraham and David, Esther and Ruth.

The writings of Isaiah and Jeremiah, Micah and Daniel.

The evangelists Matthew, Mark, Luke, and John.

The early church leaders, Peter and Paul and Timothy.

Lord, we confess that many times in our lives we simply pick and choose which teachings we want to follow. We sometimes act as if following eight out of ten commandments is a passing grade. But Lord, we know that you are a righteous and forgiving God, slow to anger and abounding in steadfast love. You do not count the sins of our lives, but offer forgiveness, new life, and second chances at every turn. Hear our prayer, O Lord, and forgive us for the many times when we fail to follow your teachings. Especially make us mindful of those times when we fail to "love our neighbor" so that we might repent and turn again to your way of love.

(Insert special prayer requests, joy/concerns here. End with the Lord's Prayer.)

CHILDREN'S SERMON

How many times has your mother or father told you, "Don't hit your brother or sister!"? *(Ask for show of hands.)* Have you ever hit your brother or sister, niece, nephew, cousin? You have? *(Show mock surprise.)* Where do you think you learned to hit another person? Have you ever seen hitting on TV, in a movie, on the playground, at school/preschool? *(Pause and listen to children's answers to all these questions.)* What happens when you hit another person? What happens when you are hit by another person? Does it hurt? Do you think Jesus wants us to hit another person? Do you think Jesus would hit us?

In the Bible, God tells us that God loved us so much that God's son, Jesus, was sent to show us the ways of God's love. Love isn't just what you *don't* do, like, "love means not hitting other people. Love means not going to war with other people." Love means peace with other people.

And God's love means positive things we *do*.

Some people have a hard time learning "not to hit." Some countries have a hard time learning "not to hit." Sometimes, wars happen because people "hit" one another. But God's teachings are not of war; they are of peace. In today's sermon scripture, the prophet Micah tells us that "nations will not learn war anymore" when they sit and listen to God.

How can we learn not to hit each other? *(Ask for ideas.)* As a Christian, as a follower of Jesus, the Prince of Peace, we can read the Bible and find that it teaches us to love one another. On the "do not do" side, that means no hitting. On the positive side, loving one another means finding good ways to be helpful, even if it isn't easy, or even if it isn't with people who are always nice to us. Grown-ups and children, and everyone in between—all of us keep trying to find God's ways to live in peace and not learn war anymore.

> Prayer: Lord, you love us, even when we hit each other. Help us to stop hitting each other. Help us to love each other and you more and more each day. Amen.

SERMON STARTER: THAT GOD MAY TEACH US GOD'S WAYS

Ask almost anyone who comes to your church on a given Sunday morning if they came to learn something, and you'd probably be safe in betting most of them did not. Be inspired? Sure. Be uplifted and feel closer to God? Sure. Be supported, affirmed, challenged, comforted? You bet. But learn something? You mean like going to school?!?

Today's reading from Micah talks a lot about teaching and learning. Yet a quick survey probably would reveal the education function of today's church is often overlooked. (This is despite the fact that historically, churches and/or denominations are the first groups of people to start organized institutions of higher learning.)

In churches today, the education function is most often relegated to the Sunday school, or to be even more specific, children's Sunday school. In many congregations, less than half of those who attend the morning worship services attend Sunday school. In some congregations, adult Sunday school classes that formed thirty, forty, or fifty years ago are still going strong, but the creation of new classes is noticeably absent. *(Suggestion: Share knowledge about your congregation's and/or denomination's Sunday school attendance patterns/figures here; use this also as a time to spotlight the critical nature of this program in your congregation. Praise the Sunday school teachers and volunteers to the highest heavens!)*

And yet, Micah says that people and nations shall one day say, "Come, let us go up to...the house of the God of Jacob; that he may teach us his ways."

The case could be argued that even if one does not come to church or worship on a Sunday morning specifically for learning, that learning nevertheless still happens. Every experience of God, every fresh wind of the Holy Spirit, opens our eyes, our ears, our hearts to something new. Thus, learning happens. If that is the case, what are we teaching ourselves here? What are we teaching new members of the congregation and visitors to church? What are we teaching our children?

In one congregation, when an infant is baptized, the pastor walks the baby through the congregation. The pastor says words about community and covenant while walking, and then adds this: "This child will grow up in this church and will be watching you and me to see if what we say with our mouths matches the actions of our lives. In everything we say and do, we will be teaching this child about what it means to be a Christian."

To paraphrase an obscene bumper sticker: "Learning happens." The question becomes: How intentional are we as a church or congregation going to be about what learning goes on here? And how intentional are we about what we don't teach? In other words, what subjects are "taboo" in your congregation? Abortion? Politics? Homosexuality? How often does capital punishment get mentioned from the pulpit? Many denominations have some sort of "social statement" or creed that guides that particular group's polity. Here's a good chance to lift that statement up in the midst of worship.

Again, Micah is helpful. In chapter 4, verse 2, Micah says that people come to the house of the Lord "that he may teach us his ways and that we may walk in his paths." What are the "ways of the Lord" that need to be taught? Love. Peace. Disciple making. Community. *(What are the particular "ways" that need to be taught in your congregation?)*

SERMON STARTER: NEITHER SHALL THEY LEARN WAR ANY MORE

One of the most famous verses in all the Bible is found in Micah 4. "They shall beat their swords into plowshares, and their spears into pruning hooks; nation shall not lift up sword against nation, neither shall they learn war any more" (v. 3).

Micah's words are clear: Instruments of destruction—swords and spears—are turned completely around and become instruments of production (farming)—plowshares and pruning hooks. Who makes this change possible? God. More specifically, it is possible when nations "come and say, 'Come, let us go up to the mountain of the Lord, to the house of the God of Jacob; that he may teach us his ways.'"(v. 2)

Where do nations learn war? Micah's words that "neither shall they learn war any more" infers that nations are currently learning war. And one could add that they are learning war away from the word of God (it is after they go to the house of the Lord and learn about the Lord's ways and walk in the Lord's paths that the nations "beat their swords into plowshares"). War can be thought of in many ways: war as combat between nations/peoples, with bombs and guns and killing; war as combat within a person (being at war with one's self is a common description for some mental illnesses); war with your spouse/children; war with your job. Clearly, these are all different kinds of "war." *(You might want to expound on any one of these "war" topics.)*

But is war a learned behavior, a learned response? Micah seems to imply it is. And if war is a learned "thing," then the opposite—peace—surely can be a learned "thing" too. *(Some denominations have statements regarding war and peace as part of their "social statement" or creed. You will want to be familiar with this statement. Here is also a good chance to educate the congregation on how these statements are developed, who writes them, who validates them, etc.)* One direction for this sermon might be to lift up the story of someone who learned peace and then paid the cost for living as a peacemaker. Traditional conscientious objectors might be mentioned, or persons who currently seek to close down the School of the Americas.

In Detroit, next door to the Central United Methodist Church and in the shadow of the baseball stadium where the Detroit Tigers play, is the Swords into Plowshares Peace Center and Gallery (33 E. Adams Ave., Detroit, MI 48226; 313–963–7575). Founded by the Reverend Jim Bristah, a

United Methodist clergy, the center provides classes for all ages on peacemaking, as well as other printed resources for congregations. But perhaps its greatest contribution to the efforts of peacemaking is its art gallery. In the humble gallery, on any given day, approximately fifty different objects of art, ranging from sculptures to paintings to photographs, are on display. Each object in some fashion is trying to make a statement about peace and/or war. Every year the peace center and gallery sponsors a juried art show that draws artists from all over the world to enter their visions of a world without war.

Jesus said, "Blessed are the peacemakers" (Mt. 5:9). How do you "make peace" as a Christian? What does it mean to be a peacemaker? Is peace simply the absence of war? What aspect of peace is justice? Consider this bumper sticker saying: "No justice, no peace. Know justice, know peace."

Offering Meditation

Most Loving God, you have filled us with blessing upon blessing. You have given to us life, life abundant, life eternal! Out of our fullness, out of our blessedness, and yes, even out of our emptiness, we are called to share—to share with one another and to share with the one in need. Give us the courage to give as we are able—to give so that we make a difference. Let us give with kindness and a generosity that begins with the gifts we have been given by God.

Invitation to Offering

Friends, we have heard the word of God proclaimed in our midst. Let us now respond to the activity of God by giving of ourselves: our tithes, our gifts, and our offerings.

Offering Prayer

Lord God, you who bless us with all good things in life: Continue to teach us your ways that lead to peace, love, and everlasting life. Grant that these our gifts, tithes, and offerings, given in response to your teaching, may be used to further your kingdom on this earth. Through Jesus Christ our Lord we pray. Amen.

COMMUNION MEDITATION

Sisters and brothers in the faith: Jesus Christ our Lord invites all who believe in him to come to this banquet table. Here the gifts of God are given to the people of God so that all may learn the ways of God and walk in God's paths. Take these gifts to strengthen you in the faith, that you may continue to beat your own swords into plowshares and spears into pruning hooks. These are the gifts of God for the people of God. Thanks be to God!

BENEDICTION

And now may the God of peace, the Lord and Savior of us all, Jesus Christ, and the power of the Holy Spirit be with you from this day forward.

Go in peace to love and serve the Lord.

Matthew 4:23—5:16

Nancy Dickinson

CALL TO WORSHIP

Come, people of God, let us worship our Creator and
Redeemer.
**We come to worship and to be renewed by God's
Holy Spirit.**
Come, all who hunger and thirst for a right
relationship with God.
**We come to be nourished by God's Word, the Bread
of Life.**
Come, all who yearn for God's peace in this turbulent
world.
**We come seeking peace for ourselves and to be
peacemakers for God's realm.**
So let us gather in God's holy presence with open and
loving hearts,
**That we may go out as disciples and servants,
empowered to offer hope and love to others.**

OPENING PRAYER

Great and Holy God, we come celebrating your goodness,
praising your presence in the world, and yearning for your
light and truth. Be with us as we sing your praises, as we
bow in prayer, and as we listen for the vision you have for us
and your whole created order. Lead us to your table to share
the bread given through Christ. May we receive your word

41

this day, so that we can offer it in new and fresh ways to the world. In the name of Jesus Christ we pray. Amen.

(Or "In the words of Jesus Christ, we pray the prayer that he taught...")

PRAYER OF CONFESSION

Loving, forgiving God, we know all your children are
created in your image, but we betray you and do
not fulfill your purposes and hopes for us. We do
not care sufficiently for brothers and sisters in our
midst, nor for those elsewhere around the world.
When many have so little,
forgive us our greed;
When children are suffering from abuse,
forgive our looking the other way;
When old people are neglected by family and society,
forgive us for turning our backs;
When brothers and sisters experience discrimination,
forgive our participation,
whether by indifference or prejudice;
When families are victims of war and violent conflict,
forgive our ignoring paths of peace;
When any of your children suffer oppression
and suppression of their human rights,
forgive our apathy and inaction.
Though we often feel little responsibility for those we
do not know or see, we know that every human
being is a child of yours. Sensitize us to the plight
of others and the ways that we can be instruments
of justice and peace, that we may be reconciled to
you and to one another. Hear our prayers, Gracious
God, and grant us your forgiveness and peace.
Amen.

WORDS OF ASSURANCE

God became incarnate in Jesus Christ to assure us of forgiveness, and to bless us in our powerlessness to earn our own salvation. Let us rejoice that God's divine love lures us to Jesus Christ, our Teacher and Savior, that we may live as disciples and as a community of faith.

PRAYERS OF THE PEOPLE

Joyfully we come to celebrate and praise you, Creator God. You have blessed us with a beautiful and bountiful earth: seemingly infinite varieties of animal and plant species, mineral and energy resources, sun for warmth and light, and sufficient water (if we are not careless). May we recognize and enjoy the endless beauty around us as gifts from you. We pray that we may also be careful stewards of all these gifts, so that our children's children may benefit.

Where all is not beautiful, O God, make us aware of our part in the world's ugliness. We pray for the earth, knowing that our carelessness and greed have caused pollution and destruction. We pray for those who eke out a living, that work may be found and fair wages paid. We pray for the children of the world, those orphaned by war or AIDS, those abused by parents or employers. We pray for those suffering physical, mental, or emotional illness. Guide the hearts and hands of all those who dedicate their lives to cure and alleviate suffering and adversity. We know that when any one of your children suffers, you suffer; when any lacks sustenance, you grieve. Merciful God, grant all your comfort, your courage, and your strength.

Holy Spirit, listen to the concerns in the minds and hearts of each one here. We especially lift up *(pause for time here for specific concerns of the congregation—or a period of silent prayer).* Relieve the stresses in our lives; lighten the burdens that we bear. Touch each of us with the assurance of your presence and your healing. Help us to be more loving and caring in our daily lives. May we witness to your love, striving for justice and righteousness throughout your whole creation. Great and Eternal God, we pray, knowing you sent your Son to show us the way of life and to bring us into your realm. Amen.

CHILDREN'S SERMON

Prop: A bowl of candy that is easily divided.

Show the bowl of candy to the children who have gathered. Explain that the candy represents the gifts that people all over the earth enjoy from God. Then divide the candy between the children, giving a minority of them many more than most of the children (who receive only two or three). Ask them how they feel about the way the candy is divided. Are they satisfied? Be sure that they know what the rest of the children have received; have them do some looking around and comparing.

Tell the children that this is the way God's gifts are divided in today's world. There are many reasons for this: wars; earthquakes, droughts, floods in many places that destroy and damage buildings and crops; unjust and unfair leaders in some countries; hot weather where people don't have the energy to work hard or cold weather where it isn't possible to work outdoors; and so on. Many people tend to be greedy, always wanting more and more, even though they don't need more. *(Add your own reasons.)*

Ask the children what they want to do about the way you distributed the candy. We hope they will want to "even it out" and share. Ask how they each feel about this. How do they feel about giving away and getting? Does it make a difference if they know redistribution is fairer? Do some like having more than others (this is a human condition, liking "power")? Remind them that in order to share and make the distribution more just, they first have to know what others have or get (sometimes we don't pay attention to poor people). Also, there has to be a way to share (have contact) and a desire to share. Some of those who receive a *lot* may just not want to share. What did Jesus teach? He told his friends that God blesses those who show mercy (not only feel sorry for but do something about their sympathy) and love to others, especially the poor. Affirm the children's willingness to share and their sense of justice. End with a prayer thanking God for Jesus' showing us how to live, love, and share, and for the children who want to be more fair.

Sermon Starter Background: Matthew 4:23—5:16

This is the beginning of what is labeled Jesus' "Sermon on the Mount," a collection of the teachings of Jesus in Matthew 5—7; Luke gives a shorter rendering of the material. Most likely it was not all one sermon, but lessons shared by Jesus on many occasions.

In this passage Jesus instructs his disciples, preaching the "good news" of the kingdom, according to the writer/editor of the book of Matthew. Jesus' teachings reflect the apocalyptic viewpoint prevalent in his day. The kingdom of God would be ushered in dramatically at the end of time, and every injustice would be righted and everyone would be blessed with the good things of life. But Jesus also preached that the "seeds" of God's reign were "among you." Thus, these teachings were also directed to his disciples (and perhaps to others who had gathered) as they followed their Master. These elements of God's kingdom were not only future-oriented, but to be sought in the present.

Jesus, his disciples, and many who gathered around him would have been able to identify with "the poor," who not only lived in poverty but were poor in spirit as well because they had little hope for improving their situations. Jesus' listeners would have been conscious of those who mourned and of their plight in society: of the chronically ill, of women whose infants died in childbirth, of the persecuted and unjustly imprisoned, of all who suffered the violence of Roman rulers. The disciples would have known people who hungered and thirsted literally for food and drink, but also those who hungered for a right relationship with God. Thus, the salvation that Jesus preached was applicable to those who heard him.

The Beatitudes, which comprise the majority of the verses in this passage, speak of those especially "blessed" or "happily favored" by God because of their current oppressed situations. These people will be (and are) blessed not just because they suffer, but because they are humble, merciful, pure in heart, persecuted for right beliefs, because they seek to be peacemakers, and because they mourn the injustices of the world. Any sermon on this passage should introduce both the apocalyptic and practical nature of Jesus' teachings. Because we yearn for and pray for God's kingdom to come on earth, these teachings have application for contemporary times.

The passage ends with instructions to the disciples to be "salt" and "light" in the world. Using these common elements, which affect taste and sight beyond themselves, Jesus bids his hearers to be salt, seasoning the lives of others as salt seasons food. Jesus affirms that they *are* the light of the world because of their calling and ministry, and that they should let their light shine out, not only giving God glory but letting others see (and hopefully imitate) their faithfulness.

SERMON STARTER

A sermon might go in many directions by highlighting the oppressed in our day, picking up on one or more of the Beatitudes. Jesus seems to say that those in troubled and depressed conditions receive God's blessings, but also that those who seek to alleviate those conditions will be blessed. Attention should be focused on both the suffering and the ways suffering is eliminated. All the Beatitudes offer concrete ideas for disciples to use in working toward the world that God envisions for creation.

Jesus blessed the peacemakers, not just the peacekeepers. Who in our society and world is making peace? We often try to solve conflict with more force, or perhaps engage in "conflict resolution." We are not as apt to look at the reasons for conflict to solve the root problems, nor are we diligent at researching and teaching the "making" of peace. One might speak about those who are merciful toward the ill or the poor, those who take action on behalf of those without hope. Concrete examples of those who are not only offering food and shelter but who are engaged in mission work to help people get on their feet can be cited. Heifer Project and Habitat for Humanity are such examples. One might speak of those who hunger and thirst for righteousness as those who work toward right relations and justice among people: toward other races, other economic groups, different sexual orientations, varied ethnic groups, and different lifestyles. Or righteousness might be focused on integrity of creation, lifting up stewardship and conservation, with attention to environmental endeavors to live within nature's balance and share the world's resources more equitably. Those who recognize the possibilities for servanthood to the "least of our brothers and sisters" will be happily fulfilled, blessed by God. We are Jesus' disciples. In what ways are we among the "blessed" by God? How do we bless others?

SERMON STARTER

A more unusual approach for the message on these verses would be to include a litany of the Beatitudes highlighting the meaning (or a meaning) of each with a contemporary illustration. For instance, the first Beatitude could be read by one person, and another person could respond with something such as:

> I am one who is poor in spirit. I was a poor laborer on the coffee plantations in northern Nicaragua when Hurricane Mitch blew its winds and rains into our mountains and valleys of the Rio Coco. A deluge of water cascaded down our hillsides, flooding our villages and destroying the coffee plantations. Only now is coffee beginning to grow again for harvesters to pick. I lost my house and most of my possessions. Fortunately, the lives of my family were spared. I am poor, and I am poor in spirit because I see little hope for my family to have a better life. It will take years to recover what we had.

After the litany of the Beatitudes, a bit of biblical background on the passage could be shared. Finally, the congregation could be reminded of the wider mission of the church to respond in both direct relief and in more systemic ways to these people mentioned by Jesus. We are part of the church, the body of Christ, attempting to carry on Christ's work, to be God's hands and hearts in the world. The Sermon on the Mount was directed to Jesus' disciples, not just individually, but as a group. This sermon speaks to us as a community of faith and bids us to join together to be blessings to others. The ending could be a reminder to be salt and light in the world, to make a difference, and to spread God's love in tangible and visible ways.

OFFERING MEDITATION

Jesus said, "Blessed are the merciful, for they shall receive mercy." Look around and see opportunities to show mercy— to members of this congregation in their individual needs, to the suffering in our larger community, and for opportunities to respond to injustices throughout the world.

Let us show mercy through the giving of our tithes and offerings.

Offering Prayer

As you have blessed us, Gracious and Giving God, we pray that these gifts we offer to you may be blessings to others. Receive them as evidence of the giving of ourselves. May we be open to occasions to share more than substance. Enable us to impart ideas and energy with creativity and passion, that your will may be done on earth, as in heaven. Amen.

Communion Meditation

During his life and ministry, Jesus dined not only with his friends but with many who were on the fringes of acceptable society: peasants of the lower class, women, tax collectors, prostitutes, perhaps even some people with contagious diseases such as leprosy. He included all in his company. Today, Jesus still invites all to his table to share with one another the nourishment that he offers. No one who desires to eat and drink at this table is excluded.

Here we who hunger for God's blessings will find the Bread of Life. We who thirst for a right relationship with God will drink the wine of the New Covenant, the covenant of God's forgiveness and love. Come, let us eat and drink with one another as the body of Christ, remembering that all are invited. Come, for Christ has made all ready.

Benediction

Let us go into the world, remembering that God calls us to be a blessing to others. Let us go with eyes open to the wounds of the world. Let us go with ears open to the cries of the suffering. Let us go with hearts open to share the love of God. Now may our Creator, Redeemer, and Holy Spirit bless us, go with us, and remain with us always. Amen.

Matthew 20:20–28

Bill Humphreys

CALL TO WORSHIP

We gather to sing our praises and offer our prayers to
God,
who has created us and called us to live life fully.
**We bring our sincere best wishes along with our
selfish desires, and present ourselves to the
wonder of this hour.**
We come together, leaving behind for a time the places
God has made for us, and the positions we have
accepted for ourselves,
to open our minds and hearts to new possibilities of
place and purpose.
**We are here, hoping and trusting that God will
continue to call us into just relationships with
others, to nurture our true sense of ourselves, and
to inspire our right relationships with God.**
Let us worship God.
All praise, thanks, and glory be to God!

OPENING PRAYER

Great and Gracious God, mighty and wonderful are your
great works of creation.

Sun, moon, and stars, even earthquake, wind, and fire
show for us the signs of your vast vision and power.

49

Even so, with the psalmist and songwriter, we affirm that you have made each and every one of us; you call us by name; you give us a place in the world; and you set before us a purpose to explore and fulfill.

We thank you for the settings of family life, friends and neighbors in community, and a place in the wide variety of gifts and needs in the world.

As we seek what is good for people we know and love, so, too, help us to work for what is good for people we do not know. Create in us clear vision and clean hearts so that we may express our great love for you through our relationships with others.

All of this we pray in the spirit of compassion and peace we know first through your full presence among us in Jesus Christ.

(And all the people are encouraged to agree with their "Amen!")

Prayer of Confession (Unison)

We celebrate, O God, that you are a God of justice and mercy, compassion and peace. You have created us to be your glad and faithful people as we live and play and work together in your wide world.

And yet, we confess that too often we live as though we worship an uncaring god. We often ignore the needs and reject the gifts of others close to us and far away. We pretend we do not see; we press on in our selfishness as if we can do nothing in service to others. Too often we simply refuse to think and act as your people, as brothers and sisters of Jesus Christ.

So we pray, O God, forgive us. Forgive us and move us to be your kind and caring people as we receive and share your great gifts to us. Lead us to be your glad and faithful people in the ministry of Jesus Christ. Amen.

Words of Assurance

Brothers and sisters, sisters and brothers in the faith of Jesus Christ, I announce to you what you already know but may have forgotten from time to time: In Jesus Christ, you are forgiven from your sinfulness and made new for life and faith! Thanks and glory be to God!

ACCEPTING OUR FORGIVENESS (UNISON)

**By the amazing grace of God, who made us; in the
sacrificial love of Jesus Christ, who saves us; and through
the persistent work of the Holy Spirit, who sustains us, we
know that we are forgiven and made new. Thanks and glory
be to God!**

*(This may be followed, as if antiphonally, by singing the
Gloria Patri.)*

PRAYERS OF THE PEOPLE

Great and wonderful God, you bless us in relationships
with families and friends. You teach us the give-and-take of
life and the value of knowing and sharing our gifts. At work
and at play, we practice our faith in your compassionate care
as we interact with friends and as we negotiate the tasks of
the marketplace, the school, and our volunteer service.

Help us, we pray, to appreciate our wide variety of gifts
and needs as we live in community with others. Help us to
know how we sometimes unwittingly judge the needy
situations of others' lives, and open our hearts and hands in
service to those from whom we expect the least credit in
return. As you have been gracious and compassionate in the
person of Jesus Christ in our midst, so may we have
something of your very heart and mind in our approach to
others.

Hear our prayers, too, O God, for ourselves. We often let
busy ideas and hurried schedules get in the way of nurturing
our own gifts. Even though you surround us with caring
loved ones, neighbors, and friends, we are often too ashamed,
too embarrassed, too timid, or too shy to ask for what we
need or to receive the gifts of others. As you would use us in
their service, open our hands and hearts to receive their gifts
to us.

For decision makers with great worldly power, and for
all people, we pray for confidence in place of despair, clarity
in place of confusion, hope in place of fear, vision in place of
ignorance, and health in place of disease. With people of faith
in all times and places, help us to know the confidence of
right relationship with you, O God. Lead us to show and

share your great love in the world, all in the name and in the ministry of Jesus Christ our Lord. Amen.

CHILDREN'S SERMON

I remember feeling both proud and embarrassed when my parents went to my school to visit with my teacher. They got together to talk about me and to visit about how I was doing in school. Did I do my homework? *(Pause for just a moment of reflection.)* Did I pay attention in class? *(Pause.)* Did I talk out of turn? *(Pause.)* Did I encourage my classmates when they did well? *(Pause.)* Did I help my classmates when they needed help?

My parents loved me. They wanted for me everything that was good. They expected me to do my share in getting along with the teacher and all my classmates. My parents were usually proud of me when they came home from visiting with my teacher, but sometimes they heard how I could do better in school.

So I was often embarrassed by hearing about those visits between my parents and my teacher. Even though I liked to know what they were saying, I was embarrassed to find out.

The Bible story we're studying today tells about the time when the mother of two of Jesus' disciples had a visit with Jesus. She asked Jesus if her two sons could have the best seats in the house, right next to Jesus, when they all had died and gone to heaven.

I wonder if that kind of question was embarrassing for the two disciples. It made the other disciples angry when they heard it. And Jesus responded in a way that made the question very difficult to answer.

But it's clear that their mother wanted the very best for her two sons.

Today we thank God for fathers and mothers who want the very best things for us, even though sometimes it's embarrassing. And we hope that we will do all that we can do to help other people. That's a way of saying thank you for everything that God and our parents have done for us.

SERMON STARTER: ALL GOD'S CHILDREN GOT A PLACE
IN THE CHOIR

Even folk who don't know "some sing lower, some sing higher" will recognize the affirmation of the title words. Having a place in the scheme of things is a geographical reality for us, being flesh and bone, three-dimensional creatures as we are, succumbing to the grasp of planetary gravity. We occupy a space. We want to know that the geography of location is also accompanied by the purpose of having a place.

I remember hearing a radio sports commentator identify the difference between a "baseball stadium" and "a ballpark." The difference is not in terms of a mailing address or street map directions; the difference is in the emotional attachments we feel about the place.

In Matthew's story about the mother's question on behalf of her sons, and in Jesus' response to its fuller possibilities, one dynamic of the question is about having a place. Explicitly, the question sounds as though she's asking about a place in the heavenly choir (and a prominent place at that!). By extension of the printed word to become a word for us today, we might hear her question and apply Jesus' response more broadly, to be about the place we occupy in life and faith.

Instead of hearing Jesus' response as a way of saying no, we might hear his redefining the terms of getting to yes. No, we don't need reserved seats at the great banquet table in the household of God. And locating ourselves geographically next to Jesus is not necessary anyway, since the presence of the fullness of God is not about geography. Rather, our place is right where we are. We are in place to serve one another and others. We are in place to be great, as a servant is great. We are in place to participate in the sacrificial ministry of Jesus Christ.

We need not pretend that our work will make us "get it right" and earn that place. We have only the work to do of accepting God's gifts, nurturing them in faith, and sharing them in service to others.

The model for such living, for turning space into place, is Jesus Christ himself. Matthew teaches that we're not being asked to live with such abandon as if we're the first to try it. No indeed! Rather, "the Son of Man came not to be served but to serve, and to give his life a ransom for many" (Mt. 20:28).

May we look more carefully at the model of Jesus and then step up to the opportunity and rightly fill our place in the choir!

OFFERING MEDITATION

This moment provides an opportunity for us to offer today's gifts as signs of our thanksgiving to God. May our gifts be used to bring to the world signs of the love and justice of Jesus Christ.

OFFERING PRAYER

Accept our gifts today, O God, as signs of our gratitude for your great gifts to us. Multiply the use of these gifts, even as you expand our thanksgiving for them. Use these gifts, we pray, and use us in faithful service in the healing ministry of Jesus Christ our Lord. Amen.

COMMUNION MEDITATION

We are both humble and bold to celebrate God's great love for us. In the continuing ministry of Jesus Christ, God has created a place for us in the world. As an act of love that includes both challenge and compassion, God continues to call us to this table. As we come, let us set aside our jealousies and inferiorities, let go of our selfish pride over accomplishments and acquisitions. Open our hearts to enjoy the fullness of God-with-us. With brothers and sisters near and far, as brothers and sisters of Jesus Christ, we are invited to "pull up a chair" at this table of our Lord and to accept the place that is prepared. Let us do so with glad and grateful hearts!

BENEDICTION

Go now from this place, not with the thought "Whew, this worship is over!" Rather go, ready to carry this worship with us. Go in the sure and certain confidence that the grace of God, who made us; the peace of Jesus Christ, who saves us; and the abiding and abundant presence of the Holy Spirit, who sustains us, go with you throughout this day, through all the days to come, and forever!

(And perhaps the people will say, "Amen.")

Matthew 22:34–40

Rebecca Button Prichard

When Jesus is asked which commandment is greatest, he quotes Deuteronomy 6: "You shall love the Lord your God with all your heart, and with all your soul, and with all your mind." In Hebrew the words are levav *(heart),* nephesh *(soul), and* m'od *(strength). In Mark and Luke the loving is fourfold—heart, soul, mind, and strength. In each case we are urged to love God with all that we are—wholeheartedly. Jesus doesn't stop there; he quotes Leviticus: "You shall love your neighbor as yourself." Loving God and loving others go together; in fact, our love for God and neighbor cannot be separated. The Shema, the great commandment of ancient Israel, serves well as a call to worship.*

CALL TO WORSHIP

Leader 1: Hear, O Israel, the LORD our God, the LORD is one. You shall love the LORD your God with all your heart,

Leader 2: And with all your soul,

Leader 1: And with all your might.

People: Keep these words that I am commanding you today in your heart.

Leader 1: Recite them to your children.

Leader 2: Talk about them—

Leader 1: When you are at home,

Leader 2: When you are away,

Leader 1: When you lie down,
Leader 2: When you rise.
People: Bind them as a sign on your hand;
Leader 1: Fix them as an emblem on your forehead;
Leader 2: Write them on the doorposts of your house and
          on your gates.
All: Hear, O Israel, the Lord our God, the Lord is one.
(Based on Deut. 6:4–9)

OPENING PRAYER

God of love, our hearts are open to you.
Savior of the world, our souls long for you.
Spirit of understanding, our minds are yours.
With open hearts and lives and minds
We welcome you;
We worship you;
We love you.
Amen.

PRAYER OF CONFESSION (UNISON)

[traditional prayer from the *Book of Common Worship*]

Merciful God,
we confess that we have sinned against you
in thought, word, and deed,
by what we have done,
and by what we have left undone.
We have not loved you
with our whole heart and mind and strength.
We have not loved our neighbors as ourselves.
In your mercy forgive what we have been,
help us amend what we are,
and direct what we shall be,
so that we may delight in your will
and walk in your ways,
to the glory of your holy name.

WORDS OF ASSURANCE

God loves us with an everlasting love.
From before all time and even now, God loves us.

Friends, believe the good news: In Jesus Christ we are
made new!
In Jesus Christ we are made whole.
Alleluia! Thanks be to God!

PRAYERS OF THE PEOPLE

Holy God, you offer us wholeness in Jesus Christ; you
teach us your truth by Word and Spirit. As you are
one, make us one—one whole, integrated body,
healthy, working together to show your love and
justice to neighbors and friends, to family and
strangers.
We pray for your church:
For this congregation, that we might love one another
as you have loved us.
For our denomination, that rifts and wounds might be
healed.
For the global church, that justice and mercy might be
shown, everywhere, always.
We pray for your world:
For peace in places where violence reigns,
especially_____and_____.
For food and drink in places where hunger reigns,
especially_____and_____.
For comfort and joy in places where sadness reigns.
We pray for our children:
For homes that enable them to grow up in love.
For teachers who instruct them in your great love.
For parents who show them they are loved.
For grown-ups who show them how to love neighbors
and strangers.
Holy God, we long to love you with all we are—heart,
mind, and strength.
Hear our prayers.
In Christ's name we pray. Amen.

CHILDREN'S SERMON

The central idea of this children's sermon is to see the
law of love, the great commandment, as a lens through which

all God's law is read. You might use the "compact" Oxford English Dictionary, in its box, with the magnifying glass in the little drawer above. (Alternately, a Bible with very small print might be used with a magnifying glass.)

Using volume 1, invite the children to look at it and see if they can read it. The print is so small that there is no way they will be able to read it. They will be able to see the headings at the top of the pages and find the word *love*. (Look up Deuteronomy 6, if a Bible is being used.) Turning to that page, and taking out the magnifying glass, show the children how it helps them to see the words on the page, to read them and make sense of them. Share the brief story of Jesus and the lawyers with the children; recite the great commandment—to love God with heart, soul, and mind and to love our neighbors as ourselves.

The magnifying glass is something like the law of love that Jesus talks about. If we try to read all the words of the Bible by ourselves, especially the laws in the Hebrew Bible, it sometimes gets hard and it seems confusing. But if we read God's law through the law of love, the great commandment, then everything else makes sense.

Sermon Starter: Love God and Do What You Please

When I was young and did something my mother thought was bad, she used to say, "It's so much easier to be good than bad." In those moments I didn't believe her (though I think I was pretty good most of the time). My mother was trying to place a positive emphasis on good behavior rather than telling me what I should not do. She realized the "should nots" quickly became temptations to disobey. "Do not tease your sister." "Do not raid the cookie jar." "Do not watch too much television." "Do not talk back."

Often obeying God seems more like a list of "should nots" and "shall nots" than a list of positive behaviors pleasing to God. "Thou shall not steal." "Thou shall not kill." "Thou shall not covet." Yet the great commandment, the one the Hebrews were to teach to their children and their children's children, the one that Jesus said sums up all the law and the prophets, is stated in the positive. "Love God," it says. "Love the Lord your God with heart, soul, and strength." "Love God wholeheartedly."

Saint Augustine was someone who found it hard to obey God. In his *Confessions*, he laments his failures and tells of his lifelong struggle with all kinds of sin. At some point, Augustine discovered the loving grace of God, the love that accepted him and allowed him to forgive himself. At some point Augustine stopped trying to avoid sin and started trying to love God. Augustine said, "Love God and do what you please." "Love God and do whatever you want." "Love God and you will want to please God."

If we read the law of God through the lens of love, through the lens of God's great love for us, through the lens of our own ability to love and be loved, through the lens of the great commandment, then the rest is easy. If we really love God, if we really feel the love of God—deep in our hearts and our souls and our very beings—then loving others will be easy, for loving God wholeheartedly means loving others wholeheartedly. Being in love with God means being in love with the world, with life, with ourselves.

Augustine got it right: Love God and do whatever you please.

And Jesus was right. It all boils down to this: Let God love you. Love God. Love your neighbors.

SERMON STARTER: HEART AND SOUL

All my life I've wanted to play the piano. When we were young we didn't have a piano, but our grandparents did. And when we went to their house we banged on the piano. We played "Chopsticks." And we played "Heart and Soul." One person played the left hand part—those repeated descending chords. After a couple of vamps, someone else played the melody—"Heart and soul, I fell in love with you, heart and soul." We got so good at that one song that we could trade parts, roll the chords, jazz up the melody, or a third person could add some chords at the top of the piano. It took a concerted effort; it took a steady rhythm; it took repetition. And I'm quite sure it drove the grown-ups crazy.

Jesus the Rabbi is asked a question by some experts in Jewish law. "Which commandment is the greatest?" With no hesitation Jesus answers, "You shall love the Lord your God with all your heart, and with all your soul, and with all your mind." And by the way, "You shall love your neighbor as yourself." These two go together.

As you know, the New Testament is in Greek, and the Old Testament is in Hebrew. We modern-day folk think much more as Greeks did than as Hebrews. We think of heart and soul and mind as three different things. Emotions, spirituality, intellect—these are separate parts of our lives. Our strength, or our body, is something else again. Our lives are compartmentalized. We work out at the gym. We go to school. We go to church. We get in touch with our feelings. We are taught to put mind over matter, to let reason rather than emotion help us make decisions. Our faith is something we keep to ourselves. Our work is something different from our home life. Our lives are compartmentalized.

The Hebrews didn't think in that way. Their words for heart and soul and strength overlap with one another. Both heart and soul have to do with emotions and will and mind-set. Both soul and strength have to do with courage and faith. All aspects of human beings are connected, and all aspects of life are connected. Work and faith and home and kinship are connected for the Hebrews. Righteousness and love and justice and mercy are interconnected.

In middle age I finally started taking piano lessons. My eyes and my mind see the notes on the page, but getting those notes down to my fingertips is a challenge. Sometimes I learn a piece by playing the hands separately. Putting them together is harder. The great commandment asks us to love God wholeheartedly—heart, soul, and strength. The great commandment asks us to see the connection between all aspects of our lives—work and church and family and play. The great commandment asks us to see the connections between loving God and being loved by God and loving others. Being in love with God is something like getting the music from the page into our fingertips—it means believing what the Bible says about God's love and feeling loved by God from our head down to our toes. Loving our neighbors is something like getting our hands to work together in harmony; it is something like getting the body of Christ to work together in concert. We are cared for and nurtured in the family of faith and we reach out to others, caring and loving, showing compassion.

OFFERING MEDITATION

> We are asked to love God with all that we are—heart, soul, strength.
> We are asked to love God before all else, above all else.
> Our love is a reflection, a response to God's love for us.
> God loves us with all that God is—heart, soul, strength.
> God loves us so much that Christ came to die for us, and to live in us.
> We give because God loves us.
> We give wholeheartedly and with gratitude.
> We give because we are asked to love our neighbors as ourselves.

OFFERING PRAYER

> Holy God, we give these gifts of love
> To strengthen faint hearts,
> To feed hungry souls,
> To support the weak,
> To show forth your love and justice.
> Receive these gifts and use them for good;
> Receive us as well, for we offer ourselves to you—
> heart, soul, and strength. Amen.

COMMUNION MEDITATION

Jesus said, "Come to me, all you that are weary and carrying heavy burdens, and I will give you rest" (Mt. 11:28).

"Come to me," Jesus said, if your hearts are weary, if you need encouragement.

"Come to me," Jesus said, if your souls are weary, if you need saving grace.

"Come to me," Jesus said, if your mind is weary, if you need peace and quiet.

In this meal, our Lord, Jesus Christ, the one who asks us to come, offers us rest and peace and refreshment.

In this meal, our Lord and Savior gives us food that satisfies us in every way—physically, spiritually, emotionally, intellectually.

In this meal, Jesus Christ, the one who died and rose again, gives us his very self—heart, soul, and strength.

Come as you are, weary or not, and find love itself.

BENEDICTION

Go now in peace, to love and serve the Lord.
And may the love of God be yours:
Warming your hearts,
Freeing your souls,
Discovering your strength.
Love God wholeheartedly!
And love your neighbor as yourself.
Amen.

Matthew 25:31–46

David Phillips

CALL TO WORSHIP

Friends, we come to worship a righteous God, who
judges fairly.
**We come to give thanks and reverence to God's holy
name.**
We listen to God's voice and eagerly seek God's
convicting and cleansing presence.
We open our hearts to the one, true, living God.
**Lord, search our hearts and see if there be any hurtful
way in us.**

OPENING PRAYER

Holy God, how we praise your name. We come eagerly
into your presence to experience your light. Reveal yourself
to us today, that we might have a clear picture of what you
are really like and know you even more fully.

We eagerly await your coming in glory, when all injustice
will be made right. Help us to see you not only in our worship
together but also in all people that we meet this next week.
May we be like Jesus in seeing the need of even the least of
those you call brother or sister. In Jesus' name. Amen.

PRAYER OF CONFESSION

Our gracious and merciful heavenly Father,
As we read your word, our hearts sense our failure and

inadequacy in understanding the needs of those around us. We get caught up in trying to make it through each day, dealing with our own pain. We fail to respond to people as you would.

We become most anxious when we realize that we are accountable to you, that we will stand before you in judgment. Who can stand before the living God? We are reminded in your word, "How can we say we love you, whom we cannot see, when we do not love our brothers and sisters, whom we can see?"

Lord, forgive us when we have failed to see you in those around us.

Forgive us for not loving as we ought and for not being as faithful with the resources you have given us as you desire. Lord, we want to be counted among the sheep, not the goats. Take the blinders from the eyes of our hearts. Hear us as we confess our sin. By your grace, we repent and seek to walk in your way. Amen.

WORDS OF ASSURANCE

Friends, the truth of God gives us assurance that when we do these things in the name of Jesus to the least of his sisters and brothers, we have done it to Him. He knows the intent of our hearts. His grace and perfect love casts out all fear of judgment. Thanks be to God!

PRAYERS OF THE PEOPLE

Dear Lord, You alone are holy, just, and righteous. You alone are God. Your word tells us "it is a fearful thing to fall into the hands of the living God" (Heb. 10:31).

But you also are full of grace and mercy that cause us to be born again to a living hope. In your wisdom and love you provided for our salvation through the giving of your only begotten Son, that whosoever believes in him should not perish but have everlasting life.

Lord, work in our hearts that we would be ever sensitive to our sin and selfishness.

Work in our hearts that we would not be ashamed to share our faith in you with others, that they might come to know you and be able to look forward to your coming.

Work in our hearts that we would see your image in those we encounter and minister to them. We lift today especially those here in *(name your neighborhood or city)*. Work in our hearts that we would understand the finality and awfulness of eternal punishment.

Lord, be with those who are hungry, thirsty, alone, homeless, ill, imprisoned.

Today we lift our prayers for _____. Fill us with your compassion. Fill them with your hope.

Be with those who have never physically experienced any of these tragedies, yet find that these words express their present spiritual reality. May each one find their way to you, who alone can meet the deepest needs of heart and soul, who alone delivers from eternal punishment and brings eternal life.

Open the eyes of our hearts that we may see even more clearly all we have in Jesus, in whose name we pray. Amen.

CHILDREN'S SERMON

Get one of your old report cards (to help show we are accountable to teachers for how we worked in school.) Make a report card with the subjects Jesus will grade us on.

How many of you cannot wait to get your report cards? I can remember being nervous, wondering what grades I would receive in different classes. Of all my grades, the one my parents looked at first was citizenship. (I am not sure that this is included in report cards today.) Citizenship included effort put into studying, into listening, into cooperating, into behaving. Sometimes my report card would say, "Daydreams in class." (I did not always pay attention.) My wife's report card would say, "Talks too much." Other times it would say, "Conscientious" or "Works hard."

The Bible tells us we will stand before Jesus and give account of our lives. Instead of arithmetic, English, and social studies, our report card from Jesus will include these courses:

Trust and faith: Have we given our lives to Jesus and trusted in him for our salvation?

Obedience: Have we cared for the hungry, the thirsty, the stranger needing a place to stay, those with no clothes, those sick or in prison, "the least of these"?

There may not be "citizenship," but there may be a category of "motive." Do we do these things because of our love for Jesus and others? Are we faithful to use what God has given us?

The grades we receive in school will someday be forgotten. But the things we do in the name of Jesus will never be forgotten.

Let's pray. Thank you, Jesus, for seeing our hearts and deepest desires. Help us to love you and to show our love by the way we treat every person we meet. Amen.

SERMON STARTER: THE PARABLE OF THE SHEEP AND GOATS

In Matthew 25, Jesus is teaching his disciples about the end of the age. He actually begins this discourse in Matthew 24, when the disciples come to him privately and say, "Tell us when will this happen, and what will be the sign of your coming and of the end of the age." After general teaching in Matthew 24, he uses three approaches in Matthew 25 to illustrate:

1. The parable of the ten virgins emphasizes the need to be prepared at all times, because we do not know when Jesus will come.
2. The parable of the talents drives home the need to be using what God has given us for God's kingdom, because we will be held accountable for the gifts.
3. The parable of the sheep and goats gives more detail of the judgment. True, many scholars do not believe that this is a parable. Yet even those who do not label this a parable recognize it has elements of a parable.

A. The dispenser of judgment, Jesus

   1. Accompanied by angels

   2. Acting with three roles

     (a) Son of Man in glory
       God in the flesh was one of us and will judge fairly.

     (b) King
       He has the authority to judge.

   (c) Shepherd separator

   When the shepherd calls the sheep, the goats do
   not respond.
   His sheep know his voice.

B. The receivers of judgment, all the nations or peoples

C. The basis of judgment

   1. Our response to Christ

   2. Our response to others

      (a) Those who bring the message of Christ

      (b) Those who are in need

D. The consequences of judgment

   1. Separation of sheep from goats

   2. Reward and punishment

E. Two results

   1. Eternal punishment for the goats

      (a) Separated from God

      (b) Cursed

      (c) Eternal fire

   2. Eternal life for the sheep

      (a) Given to the righteous

      (b) Blessed by the Father

      (c) Described as an inheritance prepared since
          creation

F. Display of God's Glory

SERMON STARTER: THE LEAST OF THESE

The parable of the sheep and goats emphasizes the
judgment that will take place when Christ returns and brings
an end to this age (Mt. 24:3). All the nations will come before
Him to be judged. The Son of Man will come with the
authority to judge and, with discernment, as a shepherd, to
separate the sheep from the goats. The sheep represent the

righteous (those who have believed and received Christ into their lives). An inheritance awaits them, one prepared since the creation of the world. The goats are banished from the presence of the king, sent to a place of eternal punishment.

Besides the goats and sheep, another group of people is mentioned: the least of these, "brothers of mine." How one responds to them is pivotal in the judgment process.

Who are "the least of these"?

Two general ideas:

1. Those who are poor and needy, oppressed by society (we've heard this sermon before).
2. Those disciples of Jesus who spread the good news in face of hunger, thirst, illness, and imprisonment. Those who receive them receive Jesus. Those who reject them reject Jesus.

How do the sheep and goats respond to the disciples?

1. The sheep minister to them in the name of Jesus; the goats do not.
2. The sheep minister with practical compassion; the goats do not.
3. The sheep minister without pretense or expectation of reward; the goats do nothing (which reveals their hearts) or ignore them (do not look after them, are too busy to pay attention, or could care less).
4. The sheep accept them; the goats reject them.

What are the consequences of the choices made?

1. Ignoring and rejection lead to eternal punishment.
2. Acceptance leads to eternal reward.

God does not overlook or forget the deeds of the righteous, though they are often unnoticed by the world. God will bring all to light to our surprise and to God's glory.

OFFERING MEDITATION

Scripture tells us that we are to bring to God our tithes and offerings. Giving ten percent of our incomes right off the top to the Lord seems ridiculous to many and impossible to others. Yet it is one way we express our faith in God's provision and our love of God. It is a source of great joy to God's people and to God. It is a declaration that money does not control us. It is a witness to the world as this money is given to spread the word in our community and the world, as we support our ministries here and our missionaries in other places. We gladly use these gifts to meet the spiritual, physical, mental, and emotional needs of people created in the image of God.

We can choose to invest our money in many avenues to meet our needs on earth: stocks, bonds, mutual funds, CDs, and so on. They have their place. But God also calls us to invest in God's kingdom, through the lives of people, that they might know God and be blessed by God through us. We live in confidence that the returns on these heavenly investments will be everlasting returns. True, we do not buy our way into heaven or work our way into heaven by doing good works, but we reflect the faith we have in Christ by excelling in good works in his name.

May the offerings received today be given out of love and concern for the glory of God as well as out of love and concern for others. Although we do not give to be noticed by others or to bring attention to ourselves, God knows, and in the day of judgment all will be brought to light for our eternal good and to glorify God.

OFFERING PRAYER

Dear Lord,

Thank your for the gift of your Son. Thanks for the gift of life that we can share with others. Thank you for the blessing that comes in giving to you and your work. We praise you for your faithfulness in providing for the needs of your children. Take these gifts and multiply them for your purposes. Amen.

COMMUNION MEDITATION

The Scripture says, "It is a fearful thing to fall into the hands of the living God." It is not a pleasant thought when we read that Jesus will say to those labeled as goats, "Go away from me! You are guilty! Go into the fire that lasts forever. It has been made ready for the devil and his angels."

As we enter into our communion, may our hearts rest in the truth that Jesus died for our sins and failures, taking our shame and guilt upon him. May we center down and draw upon his strength. Out of the quietness of this inward communion, may our hearts be open to the searching and speaking of God's Holy Spirit. In the quietness of your own heart, confess what needs to be confessed to the heavenly Father, seeking guidance for every bit of ongoing kingdom work.

Out of this quietness God may lead you to minister in prayer, in encouragement, in exhortation. You may hear the word that will minister to your brothers' and sisters' deepest needs. May we be faithful to listen to and obey our Lord.

BENEDICTION

As we leave to serve our Lord, may we go looking for the least to give them the best, confident that God will lead us in ministering to them and others.

Luke 1:39–56

Liza Lynnette Miranda Santiago

Call to Worship

Let us bless God's name as we offer a sacrifice of praise
to our merciful God.
**Our grateful hearts exalt and praise the Lord, ever
faithful to God's people.**
The Lord our God is in our midst.
**May our hearts and minds concentrate as we humbly
worship our loving God.**

Opening Prayer

Glory to you, God most high, for you are all loving and
gracious toward us. We present ourselves to you, living God,
with thanksgiving in our hearts because you are in our midst.
Eternal God, our hearts worship you. You are worthy of our
praise. Your bountiful blessings have been with us, and
you've guided us in our time of need. We are not worthy of
your grace, but we offer our lives to you as a living sacrifice
of praise. Lord, we love you and we need you. May your
Spirit fall afresh on us as we learn how to follow you
faithfully. Amen.

Prayer of Confession

Search me, O God, and know my heart; test me and know
my anxious thoughts. See if there is any offensive way in
me, and lead me in the way everlasting (Ps. 139: 23–24, NIV).

Gracious Lord,

In our life journey we strive to hear your voice and walk in your footsteps. We say we want to serve you fully and faithfully. Yet we confess that even when our hearts long to be near you and serve you, we allow our busy lives to get in the way. The pressures of our schedules and deadlines come first in our lives. Lord, we are ashamed to know that our actions, ways, and thoughts don't always profess your love. God, we are penitent and ask your forgiveness. May your grace flow, cleansing us from all our sins. God, comfort our hearts through your forgiveness so that our praises may be pleasing to you.

In Jesus Christ, our Lord and Savior. Amen.

PRAYERS OF THE PEOPLE

Loving God,

You revealed your love and mercy to us through your son Jesus. Because of his example we are called to care, watch, and love one another. So we come to you in prayer. Grant us your love, precious Lord, so that we may share it with others, ever reaching a helping hand to those in need. Strengthen us in our times of trials and tribulations. Inspire us to discern your purpose for our lives. May we seek you in times of confusion and despair, trusting you to see us through. Bring peace to those countries that settle disputes with war, and teach us how to tolerate one another even when we disagree. Provide what's needed for those who have nothing to eat, no clothing to wear, or who lack the means to support their families. Touch the lives of those in need of your anointing. May their bodies be purified and restored for your glory. But most of all, dear Lord, hear the concerns and needs of your people as we lift them up in silence. *(Pause for a few seconds.)*

In Jesus' name. Amen.

CHILDREN'S SERMON

Bring magazine photos of celebrities, including athletes, artists, writers, movie directors, singers, and well-known leaders from your denomination. These visual aids will help the children understand that we are all special in God's eyes

and that we will all serve God's purpose in our own unique
way.

Have you ever been chosen to do a task at school for a
teacher or a friend? How did that make you feel? Have you
ever been picked last for a team in sports? How did that make
you feel?

Do you know who these people are? *(Show the children
the pictures.)* Do you think these people were always treated
as celebrities or special? *(Wait for someone to say no.)* I know
that in order for them to be acknowledged as special in a
particular field, they had to go through some difficult times
in which people didn't think that they were special. I bet
they may have felt as if they weren't good at anything at
some point in their lives

Today, I want to talk about how Mary came to realize
how special she was for God. You remember Mary? Right,
she was Jesus' mom. The angel Gabriel came to tell her that
she was the one chosen to bear God's son, Jesus. A simple
woman, minding her own business, heard from an angel that
she was to be Jesus' mom. Do you think it was easy for her to
know what God wanted her to be? I don't think so. I think
she had to go through some rough times in life.

Sometimes we have rough times too. We might not be
the first ones picked for the team. We might not have lots of
invitations to birthday parties. But in other areas, no one can
deny our gifts. All of us are special to God. Maybe we won't
be great athletes, but like some of the other celebrities you
saw, you might be a great songwriter, poet, or even a minister.
We are all special in God's eyes; we look forward to serving
God's purposes in our lives.

SERMON STARTER: DOES GOD STILL REVEAL GOD'S WILL FOR
GOD'S PEOPLE TODAY?

Do an introductory exercise. Ask everyone to close their eyes
and look back at the times in their lives when they've been at
the crossroads, times when they needed to decide which way
their lives should go and they asked for God to guide them
through the time of decision making. Ask them to think

*about that thing that made them decide for a particular path.
How did God reveal God's will for their lives during that
crucial time?*

Before getting into the text, summarize what had
happened before with Zechariah and what the angel said
about John. Make sure to stress the fact that in verse 14 the
angel said the baby would bring eschatological joy and
gladness *(agalliasis)* to many. After emphasizing the prophetic
job of John the Baptist, one may be able to interpret the baby's
leap and Elizabeth's being filled by the Holy Spirit as a
preamble of John's ministry. Narrate Mary's encounter with
the angel Gabriel dramatically. Point out the fact that the
angel did not ask Mary to go visit Elizabeth. *(Consider asking
a couple of women to help you dramatize the text at this point.
This will help the congregation visualize the narrative and grasp
the encounter between Mary and Elizabeth better.)*

Once the dramatization of the text is done and the
characters are exiting, continue with the sermon. Point out
that "Mary set out and went with haste" to Elizabeth's house.
Mary only said a greeting before the story unfolds.

Some commentaries on Luke suggest that there is a
recognition of the baby transmitted to the mother. At this
time make note of the angel's prediction of John as prophet.
Elizabeth, then filled by the Holy Spirit, recognizes her
experience and gives a prophetic insight to what just
happened. Although we don't really know why Mary went
to Elizabeth's, we can see how Mary's encounter and call to
be Jesus' mother is validated or confirmed by Elizabeth's
prophetic words. Mention how the words of others serve as
prophetic insight and validation of what God has called us
to be or do. Elizabeth's prophetic insight is that she recognizes
Mary as the "mother of my Lord" and blesses the "fruit of
her womb." Verse 45 is of importance because it contains the
key to the element that transforms our lives. It is in this verse
that Elizabeth reveals what our character should be when
we are called or chosen to serve God. Mary not only believed
that the angel was sent by God, she believed that the words
of the angel would be fulfilled.

Now go back to the opening exercise. Encourage people to reflect on the many times God has called them to serve God or do God's will for their lives. Ask: How many of us were skeptical when we imagined what we felt might have been be God's voice? Wouldn't most of us ask for the bidding to be validated or confirmed? How many times were the calls confirmed and yet we didn't believe they would be fulfilled? At this point allude to the theme, "Does God still reveal God's will for God's people today?" Elaborate on the many ways in which God reveals God's will to us today. (God's word, music, through the minister in the proclamation of the word, through our brothers and sisters, dreams, and many others.) Once Mary had received the blessing of Elizabeth's prophetic words, Mary worshiped the Lord through a canticle of praise. (Notice that this canticle is at times attributed to Elizabeth but is also thought to be part of the Hebrew tradition, going back to Hannah, Samuel's mother.)

Sermon Starter: A Reason to Burst into Song

As an introduction to the sermon, start singing a song of praise that contains concepts of God's mighty acts of redemption and God's character.

When we worship God, we declare our love, admiration, and reverence to the God who is faithful, wonderful, and worthy of our praise. *(Ask the congregation to think about what we do at times when we feel joyous.)* At this time summarize what has happened to Mary from verse 39–45, how Elizabeth's prophetic insight had validated Mary as chosen. Can you imagine what that meant? Being the mother of the Messiah was the greatest of honors for any Jewish woman. That is why Mary's joy makes her burst into a song of praise. (Notice that the canticle is attributed to Elizabeth by many, who also make reference to Hannah's canticle.) In verse 45 Elizabeth uses the word *makaria* to describe the character of Mary's experience. *Makaria* is an important word; it could be translated as "happy," but the biblical meaning would be lost. Commentators make reference to this word as "blessed," which is the way Jesus used it in the Beatitudes.

In the beginning of the canticle Mary renders praise to the Lord, her Savior, and describes how her "spirit rejoices in God." Notice the importance of the word salvation *(soter)* at this point. This word was attributed to gods and rulers, therefore emphasize both concepts. Mark the use of words such as servant *(doule)* and lowliness. These are used to describe not only Mary's social status but also her spiritual submission to the Lord God, the Creator.

In the rest of the canticle, play around with the concept of Savior. The fact that this term is used for both a divine deity and a ruler is well described in the remaining verses. Mary brings to memory not only the things God has done (using God's power and scattering arrogant rulers) but also how holy God is and how God has shown God's mercy and kept God's promises from generation to generation.

In our joy, and also in times of trouble, may we burst into song, acknowledging who God is and what God has done. May we bless God for all God has promised and fulfilled in our lives. May we be able to praise God as Mary did, despite the fact she didn't know everything that was going to happen. May our praise and worship be given to God freely and without worries. After all, God is an awesome God, and that should be our reason to burst into song. Remember, God delights in the praises of God's people.

Offering Meditation

The air we breathe, the rain that falls, the skies and clouds proclaim you "Lord." The vastness of the sea, the wind blowing on the trees, let us know that you, our awesome God, are always near. Lord, we recognize that you have given us these gifts to let us know of your love. May the work of our hands and the dedication of our lives be the perfect gift offered from a grateful heart. We offer ourselves as we present our tithes and gifts.

Offering Prayer

Great God,
You are holy, and your will is perfect. Accept our gifts this morning as signs of thanksgiving from your people. Use

us and use these offerings of check and coin to help spread the good news of your love for all creation. We pray through Jesus, whose birth, life, death, and resurrection we celebrate. Amen.

COMMUNION MEDITATION

Arise, shine; for your light has come, and the glory of the LORD has risen upon you. (Isa. 60:1)

God's light has shone upon us, giving us guidance and purpose. Today God extends an invitation to come as one body to the feast of everlasting life. Let us rise to commune together as we bring our gifts to the table, and remember the new hope found in Jesus Christ.

BENEDICTION

May the God who still reveals God's will to God's people, the God who deserves all praise for being God, the God who is, who has done, and who will yet do more than we ask or think, give you the peace of mind that you need to follow God's will and the joy to fulfill it in your daily walk. In Jesus' name. Amen.

Luke 4:16–30

Edward C. Zaragoza and Marian Y. Adell

Jesus Christ preaches good news to the poor.
We come, poor in spirit, wanting to hear good news.
Jesus Christ releases the captives.
We come willing to be set free for ministry.
Jesus Christ gives sight to the blind.
**We come with limited sight, wanting to see the world
God sees.**
Jesus Christ our risen Savior is with us.
Praise the Lord!

OPENING PRAYER

God of the poor, God of the forgotten, you anointed Jesus to proclaim the good news of your realm, which includes all people everywhere. Anoint us with your Spirit, that our ears will hear the cries of the poor, and our hearts will respond to those cries. Anoint us with your Spirit, that our lips will speak on behalf of those who have no voice, to intercede when someone is causing injury to another. Anoint us with your Spirit, that our hands will bind up the brokenhearted, and our feet will go into the prisons and areas of poverty where people you love have few choices. We pray through Jesus Christ our Lord, who lives and reigns with you and the Holy Spirit, one God, now and forever. Amen.

PRAYER OF CONFESSION

Holy and merciful God, we confess that often we want to stay where it is comfortable, with people like us. We confess that too often we are like the people of Nazareth: glad when we hear that Jesus will do good things for us, but angry when we hear that you include people we do not like. Forgive us! Help us! Free us for joyful obedience, that we, too, may be good news for the poor. Free us to bring your mercy and justice into the world you love, through Christ our Lord. Amen.

WORDS OF ASSURANCE

Hear the gospel:
The saying is sure and worthy of full acceptance,
that Christ Jesus came into the world to save sinners.
    (1 Tim. 1:15)
He himself bore our sins in his body on the cross,
that we might be dead to sin,
and alive to all that is good. (1 Pet. 2:24, paraphrased)
God's love never ends; in Jesus Christ we are forgiven.
Thanks be to God!

PRAYERS OF THE PEOPLE

Gracious and loving God, we come before you this morning to pray for the courage and faith to share Jesus' cry for justice, for healing and wholeness. Help us to be open to the needs of the world and our neighborhoods as we pray:

For the poor in this country and the world. May they receive the food, shelter, clothing, and education they deserve as children of God.

For captives and the imprisoned in this country and the world. Whether they are held hostage or are being punished for a crime, may they be treated with the dignity and care they deserve as children of God.

For injured and tortured individuals in this country and the world. May they receive good medical treatment for their wounds, psychological assistance for their torment, and relief from pain and anguish, relief they deserve as children of God.

For the oppressed in this country and the world. May they be granted the political, economic, and spiritual freedoms and opportunities they deserve so that they may grow into whole children of God.

We pray for the church, that your Spirit will inspire it anew to proclaim the good news to all God's children, here and around the world. In Christ's name we pray. Amen.

CHILDREN'S SERMON

You need a package of cookie mix and some baked cookies. If practical, bring a cookie for each child present.

In the gospel lesson, Jesus went back to his hometown of Nazareth. He went to worship with his family and friends. To honor him, the leaders of the synagogue—that's similar to our church—asked him to read from the Bible. Jesus read from the prophet Isaiah, someone who had lived a long time before Jesus. We heard in the reading that God would send the Holy Spirit to empower someone to help people. This person would bring good news to the poor, set people who were enslaved free, help people see, and help people who were burdened by debt have that debt forgiven so they could begin again. After Jesus had finished reading this passage from Isaiah, he said, "Today this scripture has been fulfilled in your hearing." We understand that meant Jesus was the one who would do this. And what's more, because we are part of the church, Christ's body, the Spirit will help us do these wonderful things as well.

The words of the prophet came true that day, but they also are coming true today. Every time we hear how Jesus helps us and every time we help others live better lives, these words come true.

I want to show you how the same words can come true again and again. *(Read part of the instructions from the cookie mix. Include the part that tells how many cookies it will make. Point to the words you just read.)* These words were printed a long way from here in a factory. The words tell us about cookies. But there are no cookies until you or your mother or father or friend reads the words and follows these instructions to make cookies. These words, saying how many cookies there will be, come true every time someone reads the instructions and makes the cookies. They are fulfilled, or come true, over and over again in many different places and at many different times, whenever someone takes a mix like this and makes cookies.

The words Isaiah wrote, and Jesus read, have been printed over and over again. Today many people will hear these words. They will hear how Jesus came to save people and how we are to continue what Jesus did. The words are just ordinary words in a book. They are words that tell us what will happen, just as the words on the cookie mix tell us what will happen. When we read the words and follow them, the things they talk about will happen again.

Like the instructions for baking cookies, the words of Jesus are to be followed. When we follow them, the words Jesus spoke and acted on so long ago happen again today. God's Spirit helps us live better lives, and we in turn reach out to help others live better lives.

SERMON STARTER: OUR COMMISSION FOR MINISTRY

The image of the gospel lesson is people gathered expectantly in worship to hear the scriptures read. The setting is in a synagogue, where the service consisted primarily of prayers, a reading from God's word, the Torah, comments on the reading, and a collection for the poor. While there was only one temple, a synagogue could be anywhere there were ten men. The synagogue was not only an assembly for worship, but also a school, a community center, and a place for administering justice. Jesus throughout his earthly life was faithful to and actively participated in the observance of the Sabbath, the scriptures, and the life of the synagogue. After the prayers, the scroll of the prophet Isaiah was handed to Jesus, and he read, "The Spirit of the Lord is upon me, because [the Spirit] has anointed me to bring good news to the poor. [The Spirit] has sent me to proclaim release to the captives and recovery of sight to the blind, to let the oppressed go free, to proclaim the year of the Lord's favor." He rolled up the scroll, gave it back to the attendant, sat down to teach, and said, "Today, this scripture has been fulfilled in your hearing."

Luke places this announcement after Jesus has been baptized and been led by the Spirit into the wilderness. This announcement, at the beginning of Jesus' ministry, tells who Jesus is, what his ministry consists of, what his church will be and do, and what the response of the world will be to Jesus and then to the church.

For John Wesley, the eighteenth-century founder of Methodism, the ministry of Jesus and Jesus' church was to embody this text both literally and spiritually. Literally, to heal sicknesses, John Wesley set up medical clinics for the poor. Literally, to set the captives free, John Wesley worked to end slavery in England (and in the beginning, the Methodist societies in North America originally forbade slavery among its members). Literally, to let the oppressed go free, John Wesley set up schools and budgeting so that the poor could better themselves.

Yet this text was also spiritual, saying that people who were in patterns of death (that is, serving themselves or things before serving God) could come alive in Christ Jesus. They could learn new ways of living with God and one another through weekly class meetings of prayers, singing, and seeking to incorporate God's words of life.

The ministry of Jesus and the ministry of the church are literally to turn this world upside down. When we were baptized and when we joined the church, we got our license to minister. At our baptisms the Spirit anointed each one of us to bring good news to the poor (both the economically poor and the poor in spirit). The Spirit sends us to proclaim release to the captives and recovery of sight to the blind, to let the oppressed go free, to proclaim the year of the Lord's favor. Wow!

Bishop Peter Storey of South Africa says that too often people join churches to have the churches minister to them rather than to develop their gifts to minister to others. Bishop Storey believes it is precisely when we are in mission with the poor that we meet Jesus. He described the day that changed Bishop Desmond Tutu from a cleric who said the appropriate things to someone on fire for the justice of the Lord:

Bishop Tutu was visiting a certain black township. He noticed a child who had signs of malnutrition. He spoke with her and asked if she was hungry. She answered that she was. He asked her if there was any food at home. She answered that there was none. He asked her where she would get food. She answered that her family would borrow food from their neighbors. He asked her what she would do if her neighbors had no food. She answered that they would fill themselves with water. Bishop Tutu became so incensed that the system of apartheid would cause this little one to starve that there was a steely passion from his belly from that day forward. It was among the least that Bishop Tutu met Jesus.

God's words bring life to us and lead us to bring life to others. When we regularly gather together in worship, prayerfully prepare ourselves to hear God's word to us, expectantly listen for the word to us individually and as a community, God will bring us life. When we together seek to learn more, in Sunday or weekly classes, we become filled with God's life to share with others.

Recently, Stephen Bryant, editor of *The Upper Room*, wrote a devotion titled "The Danger of Daily Devotions." He reports that a neighbor told him her husband had begun to get up early each morning to pray and read the Bible. "Frankly," the woman admitted, "I worry that something may be wrong. Sometimes, he even kneels." As it turned out, Bryant continues, the outward change the neighbor saw in her husband was only the beginning of a wonderful transformation involving both of them.

Reading the Bible and praying can be risky. Even when our devotion is entirely experimental, prayer and scripture reading open our hearts and minds to God. They make us available to God and allow the Spirit to alter our attitudes, to influence our actions, and to make us new persons in Christ. The next time you read your Bible, try following these four steps:

1. Read the selected scripture with the desire to hear God's personal word to you.

2. Reflect on possible connections between the scripture and your own life experience.
3. Respond to God in honest and heartfelt prayer.
4. Listen for and receive God's presence and guidance for living in grace and truth.

Prayerfully, expectantly, receive God's words of life at home, in weekly Bible studies, in Sunday classes, and during worship, and we will live more in Christ and will recognize Christ living more in us.

SERMON STARTER: GOD'S MINISTRY INCLUDES EVERYONE

The first part of the text is our commission for ministry, and the second part of the text addresses who the ministry is for. As in Jesus' day, many faith communities address only the insiders and those who are "like we are." The stories that Jesus tells about Elijah and Elisha both are about God's gracious intervention to people outside the community of faith. We insiders seem always eager to limit God. But God is always pushing the limits. God says, "Pray for your enemies and those who spitefully use you." The question is, who do we name as outside of God's purview; who are our infidels? There is no one on earth to whom God does not want the good news proclaimed. There is no one on earth beyond the embrace of God. We know that, but we're uncomfortable with God bringing more people to God's self.

The world always wants to demonize people. We get angry when people say no and stand up against injustice. We placed Japanese men and women, who were citizens of the United States, in concentration camps and confiscated their businesses and properties during World War II. We ruined the lives of socialists during McCarthyism in the 1950s, and woe to anyone who defended them. For many people today, homosexuality places some outside the care of God. However, the church's place is to stand up against the mob, even to the point of having its life threatened. As Jesus was, the church continues to be in ministry. Evil and hate cannot kill it. The last word is not the cruelty and torture of the cross;

the last word is the resurrection and the power of God's love to triumph over evil and hatred, to triumph over death.

OFFERING MEDITATION

Christ invites us to participate in God's mercy and justice. We are to bring good news to the poor; we are to proclaim release to the captives and recovery of sight to the blind; we are to let the oppressed go free; we are to proclaim the year of the Lord's favor. May we dedicate ourselves and our tithes and offerings to this mission of Christ's body, the church.

OFFERING PRAYER

Gracious and merciful God, bless these tithes and offerings. May your Spirit move through them to bring the reality of your freedom and the reality of your justice to all areas of this world, whom you sent your Son to save. Amen.

COMMUNION MEDITATION

This is not a *(name of denomination)* table. This is the Lord's table. Christ, our Lord, invites to his table all of us—the poor, captives, blind, and oppressed in body, mind, or spirit—to join him for this feast.

BENEDICTION

May the grace of our Lord Jesus Christ open your eyes to the needs of the world. May the love of God open your hands to those hurting around you. And may the fellowship of the Holy Spirit set you free from isolation and indifference. Go now and proclaim the good news! Amen.

Luke 10:25–37

Judy Fackenthal

Call to Worship

Leader: We shall love the Lord, our God
People: With all our hearts,
Men: With all our souls,
Women: With all our strength,
Leader: With all our minds,
All: And we shall love our neighbors as we love ourselves.
Leader: To love, we must encounter love. Come, worship the God of all love.

Opening Prayer

God of love and mercy,
We come before you with worshipful hearts, souls, strength, and minds. Take us as we are: victims of injustice and despair, robbers of truth and deed, delegates of denial and avoidance, and neighbors of hope and possibility. Mold us with your love as we worship. Reveal to us the grace you have given in Christ Jesus. Transform our minds by the renewing of your Holy Spirit within us. Bless us that we may be blessings to you and your creation. Amen.

Prayer of Confession

Holy and just God,
You pour out healing and salvation upon those this world

89

leaves beaten along the roadside of life. Forgive our participation in abandonment. Forgive our betrayal of your love when we abuse with our ignorance. Forgive us for establishing stereotypes and boundaries of race, gender, religion, and economic class. Time and again we attempt to test you, Lord, to put questions before you that serve our self-centered will. We hear your word, yet set aside what is uncomfortable. We declare love for you, yet refuse to act with compassion and care. Our sin leaves us beaten and in need of your healing power. So we come seeking your forgiveness, which will lift us up. Amen.

WORDS OF ASSURANCE

In the name of Christ, who knew abuse and abandonment, your sins are forgiven.

Rest assured in his marvelous mercy and love.

PRAYERS OF THE PEOPLE

Giver of life, Creator of hope, Counselor of wisdom, hear our prayer. Amazement and awe leap from our hearts as we celebrate your transcendent power. Peace and purpose stir our souls as we rejoice in your unending love. With all our strength we praise your holy name. With our minds we marvel at the mystery and depth of your compassion. We give you thanks for your love and care. Gratefully we acknowledge your gift of salvation graciously given in Jesus Christ, your son.

We pray this day, O Lord, for the victims of our world:

For those who are robbed of innocence through rape
 and abuse,
  we pray your mercy.
For those who have been beaten by oppressive
 systems, governments, and communities,
  we pray your mercy.
For those on the margins of society who face exclusion
 and disdain,
  we pray your mercy.
For those wounded by injustice and hate,
  we pray your mercy.

We give you thanks this day, O Lord, for those who are "Samaritans" in our time. Grant us to see the face of Christ in everyone who defies boundaries of race or culture. Guide us with your Holy Spirit so that we might also be a neighbor to those in need. Open our hearts to your transforming power. In the name of Christ, we pray. Amen.

CHILDREN'S SERMON

Early in the week, contact some children and ask them to pantomime the story of the good Samaritan as you read it. It might be helpful to put the story in a modern context; create your own or use *The Cotton Patch Version of Luke and Acts*, translated by Clarence Jordan (New York: Association Press, 1969). Rehearse before worship so there are no surprises. During worship do this pantomime with the children. Stop the narrative just before the man answers Jesus' question, "Who was the neighbor?" Let the children answer, then discuss how other people would not have liked the Samaritan. Talk with the children about what makes a good neighbor. (Jesus knew that anyone who helped another person was a good neighbor. Jesus did not care what they looked like, how old they were, or where they were from.) Help the children realize that they can be good neighbors and that they have people around them who are good neighbors. Use some examples from your community. Jesus said "Go and do likewise" to the man who asked him the question. Tell the children they can "go and do likewise" by being a good neighbor to people they meet.

Close in prayer: "Lord, thank you for neighbors, people who help and show your love to others. Help us to be neighbors to your world. Amen."

SERMON STARTER: EXPOSITORY

Sermon sentence: God calls us to defy boundaries with activated love.

Introduction

In her epic novel *The Poisonwood Bible* (New York: HarperFlamingo, 1998), Barbara Kingsolver takes us to the depths of the Congo with an American missionary family. Her work addresses the imperialistic attitude of some mission efforts and attempts to force indigenous people into Eurocentric customs, behaviors, and lifestyle. The missionary family (a preacher father, his wife, and four daughters) clearly depicts their expectations by what they bring with them to the Congo. Each family member is allowed one piece of luggage. Since those quickly are filled, they manage to tape and tie onto their persons such "essentials" as silverware, household items, and an angel food cake mix. Once the family arrives they begin the process of spreading Christianity and setting up house, American style, without regard to the customs and culture of the Congolese people. Every offer of assistance from villagers is discounted as heathen and unacceptable. They reject the food of the people, the infrastructure of their village life, and the kindnesses shown to them. So they struggle through hardship, mental disorder, and death.

The family in this story strongly resembles the lawyer who came to Jesus asking, "What must I do to inherit eternal life?" Their worldview and the boundaries of their interpretation of the faith limited them. In their zeal to convert and Americanize, they were unable to know and love their neighbor.

Development

You might want to develop the sermon around all the characters in the text (be sure not to omit all those gathered around Jesus as he told this story). By looking at the characters, we can see how our lives intersect with theirs. We also can notice through their prescribed boundaries and rules of acceptability how we live according to the dictates of culture and custom.

Lawyer: lived by the code of law. In his view of society, judicial law is equivalent to religious law. He asks Jesus the question in verse 25 to test or push Jesus' honor and integrity to what he has been teaching. Jesus calls on the lawyer's expertise in the law by answering with the question, "What is written in the law? What do you read there?" (v. 26). The lawyer continues a game of cat and mouse by responding with the teachings given to the people of the covenant in Deuteronomy 6:5 and Leviticus 19:18. When Jesus applauds his answer and commands him to live according to the teaching, the lawyer throws out another question: "Who is my neighbor?" The lawyer has a worldview created by solid boundaries for what a person of Israel could and could not do. There were prescriptive ways to treat persons outside the Jewish tradition as well as the ways in which gender, economic, and religious status differences should be treated. Imagine how he must have felt after Jesus told this story. He could not bring himself to say "Samaritan" but only responded to Jesus that the one who showed mercy was the neighbor. Jesus shattered his worldview and opened a way for him to see others with God's love and compassion.

Victim: a very generic person. He is the one in need. Probably everyone in your congregation can see himself or herself as a victim of some sort. Would we deny assistance from someone because we do not value the person's race, gender, background, culture, or status? Or would we willingly accept help from anyone who shows compassion toward us? If we are able to see our own need for justice and mercy, God will enable us to recognize and love our neighbor whom we might view as unacceptable.

Samaritan: A despised "half-breed" from the intermarrying of Israelites and Assyrians. Is anyone in your congregation on the fringe of acceptability in our culture? How have they been Samaritans? Where have we received kindness, mercy, assistance, and hope? Who shatters our expectations? Who will defy boundaries for compassion's sake?

Levite, Priest, and Innkeeper: Use your creativity to continue exploring the participants in this text

When we see ourselves as participants in the story, we are ready to meet our neighbors. God's realm calls for a breaking down of boundaries; an unraveling of stereotypes; a building up of love, tolerance, acceptance, and justice.

Conclusion

A young man lay dying of complications from AIDS. He asked a pastor whom he'd met only once to speak at his funeral. The pastor used this story of the good Samaritan. She spoke of how the young man fit the role of Samaritan. His lifestyle choice went against what was acceptable by much of society. The young man had a heart of compassion, a soul of deep faith, a strength that put words into action, and a mind that noticed needs and responded to them. He had been a neighbor to many during his short life. She went on to say the young man also fit the role of the victim. He had been robbed of life by immune deficiency. Zealots had stripped him of justice. He was left lying in the road. Who would be his neighbor? Who would defy boundaries to offer the healing oils of God's love? Who would treat his wounds with the wine of grace and mercy in Christ Jesus? Who is a neighbor?

SERMON STARTER: DRAMATIC NARRATIVE

Select a character from the text and portray that character through a monologue.

This example uses the innkeeper as the speaker of the monologue. Keep true to the text by telling the story from the perspective of the victim, just as Jesus did.

> Shalom! Greetings in the name of our Lord! I have come to tell you about the day when a most peculiar thing happened, a day when I saw kindness and mercy from one whom others thought was an abomination, a day I learned what a true neighbor is.
>
> It was like this...I had been hard at work all day. You see, I own and operate the Jericho Inn. My wife and I have run the place for years. We have a few rooms to let, usually for half a denarius a night. The rooms aren't much to brag about, but they are clean and tidy. Besides, with the room comes a meal in the large gathering area. Now the meal, that is quite a treat. My wife and her maidservant cook up the best mutton stew in all of Jericho. Our guests generally

are exhausted by the time they reach our inn. The road from Jerusalem to Jericho is extremely dangerous. Robbers hide behind the huge boulders and ambush travelers. Many a poor soul has been discovered wounded or dead along the Jericho road.

Let's see…Oh yes, the day I was telling you about. It was getting late, near evening, and a man approached the inn with his donkey trailing behind him. I noticed a bundle on the donkey's back. As they drew nearer I saw that the bundle was a man. He was bleeding severely, though the man who brought him had cared for his wounds. As I helped the owner of the donkey get the man down I saw in his face that he was not from Israel or Judea. The man was a Samaritan. I marveled that he was not the wounded one. Samaritans are despised around here. People consider them half-breed Jews who have mixed their religion as well as their blood with the wretched Assyrians. Most folk will cross to the other side of the road to avoid passing a Samaritan. In fact, most will pass all the way around Samaria to avoid them. Me? Well, I'm an innkeeper. I make my living from those who come to me. When I turn a man away, I am turning away his coins. I take Samaritans at my inn.

Anyway, the Samaritan and I took the wounded man inside, and the Samaritan gave me two denarii to care for the man until he returned.

That night my wife and I nursed the man's wounds and bathed his feverish body. By morning his fever had broken, and he began to tell us his story.

(Complete the story of the robbers, the Priest, and the Levite as if the man had told it to the innkeeper.)

Conclude with the innkeeper stressing in amazement that a Samaritan, of all people, had come to the aid of the man in need. Keeping in character, tell how the Samaritan showed the innkeeper what it meant to follow the teaching of the law (Deut. 6:5 and Lev. 19:18). Have the innkeeper describe the Samaritan as a faithful man. As innkeeper, encourage your listeners to show love for God and self by loving neighbor, be that neighbor someone of a different race, culture, or lifestyle. Encourage them to break boundaries with mercy just as the Samaritan did.

Offering Meditation

Jesus asked, "Which of these do you think was a neighbor?" The man replied, "The one who treated him kindly." God invites us to be neighbors, to bring healing and hope to those in need. God desires us to be neighbors, to treat kindly each person we encounter. Know clearly that in your giving, others may experience justice and love. So in this hour, be generous with your gifts and your identity as a neighbor.

Offering Prayer

In thanksgiving for your love in Christ Jesus and your sustaining comfort in the Holy Spirit, we offer up our lives and gifts to your service, Holy God. Accept them as the innkeeper accepted the Samaritan's coins, that they might be used to bring healing and justice to the wounded and weary. Amen.

Communion Meditation

This is the table of the Lord. Here we share with our neighbors—transcending boundaries of culture, age, gender, lifestyle, and race—through the breaking of the bread and sharing of the cup. Come to the table. Our Lord has made all things ready. In Christ, come share grace and peace with your neighbors.

Benediction

God of neighbors far and near,

Send us forth, defying boundaries of our world. Send us forth loving you, loving neighbor, and loving ourselves. Send us forth with hearts of compassion, souls of faith, strength to be active, and minds to create solutions for needs. Go forth and do as the Samaritan did. Amen.

Luke 16:19–31

David Kinsey

CALL TO WORSHIP

(Use with first sermon starter.)

Praise the LORD, O my soul; all my inmost being, praise
his holy name.
**Praise the LORD, O my soul, and forget not all his
benefits—**
who forgives all your sins and heals all your diseases,
who redeems your life from the pit and crowns you
with love and compassion…
**The LORD works righteousness and justice for all the
oppressed…**
The LORD is compassionate and gracious, slow to anger,
abounding in love…
He does not treat us as our sins deserve or repay us
according to our iniquities.
**The LORD works righteousness and justice for all the
oppressed.**
For as high as the heavens are above the earth, so great
is his love for those who fear him;
as far as the east is from the west, so far has he
removed our transgressions from us…
**The LORD works righteousness and justice for all the
oppressed.**

Praise the LORD, you his angels, you mighty ones who
do his bidding, who obey his word.
Alleluia.
Praise the LORD, all his heavenly hosts, you his
servants who do his will.
Alleluia.
Praise the LORD, all his works everywhere in his
dominion. Praise the LORD, O my soul.
Alleluia.

(From Ps. 103, NIV)

(Use with second sermon starter.)

Have mercy on me, O God, according to your unfailing
   love;
according to your great compassion blot out my
   transgressions.
Wash away all my iniquity and cleanse me from my
   sin.
**Create in me a pure heart, O God, and renew a
   steadfast spirit within me.**
For I know my transgressions, and my sin is always
   before me.
Against you, you only, have I sinned and done what is
   evil in your sight,
so that you are proved right when you speak and
   justified when you judge.
**Create in me a pure heart, O God, and renew a
   steadfast spirit within me.**
Surely you desire truth in the inner parts; you teach me
   wisdom in the inmost place.
Cleanse me with hyssop, and I will be clean; wash me,
   and I will be whiter than snow.
**Create in me a pure heart, O God, and renew a
   steadfast spirit within me.**
Do not cast me from your presence or take your Holy
   Spirit from me...
Then I will teach transgressors your ways, and sinners
   will turn back to you...

**O Lord, open my lips, and my mouth will declare
your praise.**
You do not delight in sacrifice, or I would bring it; you
do not take pleasure in burnt offerings.
**The sacrifices of God are a broken spirit; a broken
and contrite heart, O God, you will not despise.**
(From Ps. 51, NIV)

OPENING PRAYER

Most loving and holy God,
We thank you for this day and all of the blessings you
have given to us.
We thank you for the freedom and ability to gather
together in fellowship with friends and worship you.
We thank you for your church.
Prepare us now to worship you completely.
Take from us, for a time, our cares and concerns for
loved ones and for your creation, that we might
focus solely upon you.
We confess our sins. Cleanse us and make us vessels
worthy to receive your Holy Spirit.
Open our ears, that we might hear.
Open our minds, that we might understand.
Open our hearts, that we might be filled to overflowing
with your love.
In Christ's name. Amen.

PRAYER OF CONFESSION

Lord of grace and mercy, we ask your forgiveness for
what we have not done.
For the sick and imprisoned whom we have not
visited,
For the hungry and thirsty to whom we have not given
food and drink,
For the lonely whom we have not comforted,
For the oppressed with whom we have not suffered,
For the evil we have not opposed and the good we
have not accomplished,

We beseech your forgiveness.
As we have been transformed by your grace,
Grant that we may seek to transform the world.
Soften our hearts to the suffering of your creation;
Open our ears to the cries of your people;
Quicken our hearts and hands for your service;
Loosen our tongues to proclaim your gospel.
All of this we ask in your name and for your glory.
Amen.

WORDS OF ASSURANCE

God is gracious, and eager to forgive those who seek to
be reconciled to God. Accept the good news: In Jesus Christ,
you are forgiven!

CHILDREN'S SERMON

Items needed: A pitcher of water, a cup, a large pot of soil

Have the pitcher of water, the cup, and the pot of soil on
a table. Make sure the pot of soil is large enough to hold all
the water in the pitcher. Tell the children, "I'm thirsty." Ask,
"What should I do?" *(Children may say, "Have some water.")*
Start pouring the water into the pot of soil while complaining
you are thirsty. "What should I do?" *(Children may respond,
"Use the cup.")* Do not pick up the cup until the pitcher is
empty. At that time place the cup under the spout of the
pitcher and try to pour some water. "Why is the cup still
empty?" Explain that sometimes it is too late to do good.
Say, "We need to be nice to one another and love and forgive
other people right away because we may never get another
chance. God wants you to do good every day. What ideas do
you have about how you can do good?" *("We can tell people
about Jesus." "We can share our toys." "We can do our chores.")*
End with a prayer asking God to help us to do good whenever
we can.

CHILDREN'S SERMON

*Items needed: Colorful cardboard signs (No smoking, detour,
stop, danger, keep out, etc.)*

Ask the children, "What do I have?" (*Children may answer,* *"Signs."*) "What are they for?" Talk about the different signs and what each tells us. Ask what happens when people ignore the signs. (*Responses might be, "People could get hurt, get in trouble, have accidents."*) Ask if more signs would help people obey better. Explain that they probably would not help, because some people choose to ignore signs and warnings. "God wants us to do some things; how can we know what God wants us to do?" (*Possible answers: "Talk to our parents, Sunday school teachers, or pastor"; "pray"; "read the Bible."*) Explain that we do not need a new sign to know what God wants us to do. If we read our Bibles, pray, and talk to other Christians, we can know what God wants. End with a prayer asking for God's help to know what God wants us to do.

SERMON STARTER BACKGROUND: LUKE 16:19–31 EXEGESIS

The name Lazarus is a derivative of Eleazar, which means "The Lord is my help." Some commentators name the rich man Dives from the Vulgate for "rich." This is an exegetical mistake. As is his habit, Jesus is turning the expected social order around by having a named beggar and an anonymous rich man. (We would likely construct the story by telling about the nameless beggar at J. P. Morgan's doorstep.)

Lazarus was laid at the rich man's gate. In the biblical tradition the gate was the place where justice was transacted. Lazarus finds no justice at the rich man's gate. In Proverbs 22:22 and Amos 5:12 we find warnings and accusations about the treatment of the poor in the gates where they have come seeking justice.

His only dubious comfort was that the dogs came and licked his sores. Are these the same dogs that ate the scraps from the rich man's table for which Lazarus longed? Dogs were regarded as unclean animals. Dogs licked up Ahab's blood (1 Kings 22:38), and Jezebel was eaten by them (2 Kings 9:36). In the mind of Lazarus and the ears of Christ's audience, their attention might have been seen as a sign of divine disfavor.

Lazarus is carried to Abraham's bosom by angels; the rich man is buried. For the hearer, Lazarus's lack of burial would have been a disgrace. The rich man would have had a great burial, perfumed with expensive spices, decked out in his finest clothes, with paid mourners and all the proper prayers. But again Jesus turns things around. Lazarus receives God's favor and is carried to Abraham's bosom by angels. The rich man dies and is put in a hole in the ground.

The rich man, from the torments of hell, sees Abraham and Lazarus. "Send Lazarus to help." Even in hell, the rich man does not condescend to speak to Lazarus as to an equal. Instead, he asks Abraham to command Lazarus as he might have sent one of his own servants.

"Between us there is a great gulf fixed. Those in torment cannot escape to paradise. Those in paradise cannot aid those in torment even when they so wish."

"Send Lazarus to my brothers." This implies that he, like his brothers, did not know that he should have acted any differently toward Lazarus. He wants them to be warned.

"They have Moses and the prophets." Abraham refutes his argument. Mosaic Law calls for the care of the poor (Deut. 24), and the prophets emphasize it as well (Hos. 6:5).

"Neither will they be persuaded if one rise from the dead." One returning from the dead will not convince those who refuse to believe the truth as found in Moses and the prophets. Herod is a New Testament example, for he thought that Jesus was John the Baptist returned from the dead, and he was perplexed, but he did not repent (Lk. 9:7).

Sermon Starter: While It Is Yet Day

Sermon in a sentence: "As a response to God's blessings we must take advantage of our opportunities to do justice when they present themselves."

The good news: "Opportunities to do justice are at our very gates."

Other scriptural support: Matthew 25:31–46 (That which you did not do to the least of these…).

Illustrations: There are many possible illustrations for this theme. Anything involving a deadline can be used to illustrate the point that many of our opportunities to do good will disappear if we do not act on them in a timely manner.

In the age of sails, ships always sailed with the tide. If they missed a favorable tide, they might have to wait days until they could leave port. Skilled captains knew when the best time to set sail was and did not delay when it was time. Even today, with all our technological advances, NASA scientists must find the best window of opportunity for space shuttle launches.

A quick reading of the local paper will illustrate the volume of opportunities to do good that surround us. Encourage people to see the "bad news" in the daily paper as opportunities to serve God in the present moment. What would a life lived in this way look like? It would perhaps mirror the life of the nineteenth-century Quaker missionary Stephen De Grillet, who traveled the world preaching the gospel. De Grillet declared, "I shall pass through this world but once. If, therefore, there be any kindness I can show, or any good thing I can do, let me do it now…for I shall not pass this way again."

Caveat: Be aware of the temptation of preaching works righteousness. Care for the poor is never to be seen as a means of grace. It is a response to grace.

Sermon Starter: No Sign Suffices

Sermon in a sentence: "There is no sign that can convince someone who does not want to believe."

The good news: "Christ frees us from our self-delusions if we allow Him."

Other scriptural support: John 3:19–21 (Love of darkness). Matthew 16:1–4 (There will be no sign).

Illustrations: People tend to believe what they want to believe. Take crop circles, those strange geometric patterns that appear by night in farmers' fields. Pranksters have come forward and shown how they produced these patterns with ropes and boards. The "experts" who have been studying the phenomena for years by seeking psychic forces or alien communications refuse to believe that all crop circles are man-made. The weight of evidence will not convince them because they have invested so much of themselves in their erroneous belief.

There are numerous accounts of persons being divinely convicted of the falseness of their belief, not through signs, but through transformation by the Holy Spirit. John Newton, the author of "Amazing Grace," was a slave trader before being convicted of his sins and writing that famous hymn.

Caveat: Beware of the danger of anti-Jewishness. It is so easy to say that the Jews had Moses and the prophets but refused to see that Jesus was the Christ. (This may even be the point that Luke intends to make.) The lesson for the Christian is not about the failure of the Jews to see the signs, but rather about the ineffectiveness of signs to compel belief.

OFFERING MEDITATION

The rich man had an abundance of goods and wealth beyond measure. Yet he did not see the needs of the man who sat just outside his gate. This story comes close. Many of us would deny being rich, yet we know abundance is ours as we look around the world, or even around our own community. Today we have an opportunity to reach within our hearts and wallets to share our abundance with those in need. Consider writing an additional check or putting in a large contribution designated for outreach, as you close your eyes and remember those who are just outside our gates.

OFFERING PRAYER

Most Gracious Lord, we come before you now to present our tithes and our gifts. We give them cheerfully in thanksgiving for the many blessings you have given to us. We recognize we have been blessed beyond what we deserve. Your gifts are not ours to keep, but ours to use in service for you. Lord, we ask that these offerings might be a pleasing and acceptable sacrifice to you. Bless and multiply these gifts and guide us in their use, that we might use them wisely and well, according to your will, for your kingdom and for this your church. Amen.

COMMUNION MEDITATION

When Christians gather, the warmth and wealth of silence bring each to a rich feast. At this table, all are welcome. Here, there is no distinction between the poor and the rich, or the blind and those who see clearly. Come to know the mercy of our God.

BENEDICTION

> God of Mercy and Compassion,
> Open us to the cries of your people.
> Move us to service and sacrifice.
> Grant us peace, that we might wait upon your will.
> Grant us wisdom, that we might learn your will.
> Grant us courage, that we might do your will.
> Hold us ever in your love, in Christ's name. Amen.

Philemon

Lucy Rupe Watt

CALL TO WORSHIP

Grace and Peace to you, sisters and brothers.
**Grace and Peace to you, (*use sister or brother as
appropriate*).**
We gather to once again refresh our hearts and be
challenged by the good news of the gospel.
**We gather to grow in our love for one another, the
saints of yesterday and today.**
We come to offer praise and thanksgiving to God.
**We come to strengthen our faith and renew our
spirits. Let us begin!**

OPENING PRAYER

God of Paul and Apphia,

We lift up the saints of old who strove to live in
faithfulness to you. Paul, though imprisoned, continued to
encourage others such as Timothy, Onesimus, and Philemon.
Apphia was mentioned only by name, yet remembered as
sister and leader. Grant unto each of us the courage and
resolve to enter this time of worship with ears to hear the
gospel and hands to activate the love and justice of the gospel.
Amen.

Prayer of Confession

God of all prisoners,

Forgive us for glibly lifting up in prayer those held captive by bars of metal, men and women we quickly judge guilty and deserving of punishment. Instead of human comfort, the label "prisoner" and a number are their constant companions. By locking cells, we on the outside rest secure, believing the problem is solved. We turn the key, shake our heads in pity, and pass by on the other side, hoping someone else will do something for those poor souls.

Forgive us for constructing invisible walls of confinement around those we consider unacceptable to society. Especially we are mindful of people known only as the uneducated, unemployed, homeless, poor, mentally ill, and victims of countless abuses. Rejection from the flow of daily life leads to solitary confinement of heart and soul. By the identification of "bad," "unfit," and "deadbeat" we dismiss any sense of responsibility and place blame upon those least able to break the ever-tightening cuffs of condemnation.

Forgive us for our self-imposed cells of isolation. We choose to remain distant from those who challenge our comfort zones. By remaining silent and uninformed we condone injustice and stay shackled by our prejudices and inactivity.

God of all people, forgive us! Break our self-satisfied chains of bondage. Warm our cold hearts. Set us free to claim justice for all. Amen.

Words of Assurance

People of God, refresh your hearts; listen to these
wonderful words of assurance:
Christ lived, died, and lived again in order for us to be
freed from bondage.
Believe this good news; in Christ we are forgiven.
Go from this place to live and tell this amazing truth.
We are forgiven! This is indeed grace upon grace.

Prayers of the People

God, lover of our hearts,

We want to believe that we have set aside the evils of slavery that have marked the history of many lands both ancient and modern. Yet if we are honest with ourselves, we know these practices greatly influence the way we treat others, especially those with skin of varied hues. Today we give thanks for leaders past and present who hold up the vision of the realm of God. We thank you especially for people such as Harriet Tubman, Sojourner Truth, Langston Hughes, Booker T. Washington, Ella Fitzgerald, Desmond Tutu, Oprah Winfrey, Nelson Mandela, Toni Morrison, Colin Powell *(list names meaningful to you and your congregation)* and the nameless others who have fought both silently and loudly for the rights of all peoples, regardless of the color of their skin.

Today we ask you to open our minds to the teachings of Paul. Help us to learn from his friendships with Onesimus and Philemon. Teach us to have hope in the possibilities that exist in forming relationships with folks we have considered "the other" (those who look different, speak different, act different). Give us the courage to step forward to learn more about Alzheimer's, AIDS, poverty, domestic violence, health care, and other human conditions. Then take us beyond knowledge to action, and through action to change that is life enhancing.

Lead us to active, alive relationships, not those stagnant and worn out with ancient prejudices and tired clichés.

Good God,

We pray for world leaders who struggle and fight for justice causes.

We pray for those forsaken by family and friends because of their beliefs in the rights of all people.

We pray for those targeted by institutions and publicly defamed.

We lift to you those preaching by word and deed that all are one in Christ.

We pray for those persons who put their lives on the line in order that people might be free to live life abundantly.

Particularly we remember the martyrs of old:

John Huss, Joan of Arc, Dietrich Bonhoeffer, Martin
  Luther King, Jr.,
and the nameless martyrs of today found in Rwanda,
  Oklahoma, Israel, Colorado, Guatemala, New York,

Afghanistan, Pennsylvania, Washington D.C., and
the list goes on.

Show us the path of freedom in our communities.

Help us be a voice for the voiceless.

Enable us to open our eyes to injustices as close as our
fences.

Give us the courage to use our lives by volunteering at
the local elementary school,

or the nearby soup kitchen, or the county jail,

and in so doing, provide the heart of a caring person
to one who is in need.

Push us beyond dropping a dollar bill in a box and
believing we have solved the problem of domestic violence
in our neighborhoods.

Take us to the emergency shelter to offer our time.

(List opportunities for ministry in your own community.)

Most of all, God, we pray not to be so overwhelmed by
human need that we remain within the protection of our own
households and never risk the joy of human encounter as a
sister, as a brother.

As hearts of your heart, grant us such courage and joy in
Christ that we will delight in partnering with you to provide
hospitality to all your children. Amen.

CHILDREN'S SERMON

*Ahead of the service prepare a cutout heart with fitted envelopes
for each child and place them in a basket to pass out. When all
the children have received their hearts and envelopes, hold up a
large heart for all the congregation to see.*

Good morning to all of you. I hope you are well and
happy to be with all the fine folks of *(name of the congregation)*
this morning.

In your hands each of you is holding a heart and envelope
similar to the one I hold. What time of the year do we usually
see more hearts than any other time? *(Valentine's Day will
probably be the most popular answer, but Christmas and birthdays
might also be mentioned.)* Great! You are sharp as always.

Now I want you to think along with me as we take
a deeper look at the scripture for today. This man named

Paul—he did a lot of writing—he particularly wanted people like us to know how very much he, Paul, loved Jesus. It was his love of Jesus that helped him love others.

In this book of the Bible, which is really a letter to a man named Philemon, Paul writes about his friend Onesimus as his own heart. I don't know about you, but what I think this means is Onesimus was such a good friend that Paul was concerned about him as much as he was about himself.

Can you think of one of your family members or friends you could call "your heart?" While you are thinking, I will tell you about one person I might label as "my heart."

My friend's name is Lynn. She lives in Wisconsin. She is a person I can call on the phone and tell that I am having a wonderful day. During calls like this we can laugh together. At other times I have called her with sad news, and together we have cried. When I read the scripture for today, Lynn came to my mind.

OK, you have had some time to think. Would some of you like to say the name of a person whom you would call "my heart?"

Thank you! Now I have one further request. When you get home today, please either give or send your paper heart to a special person in your life. If you want to write something on the heart, that would be great, or you can simply write your name or have someone else write your name. In this way you are telling another person you love them very much. I am going to send my heart to Lynn.

I am so glad you are here today, for each of is a "heart" of this congregation. By being together we all learn how to more deeply love God, ourselves, and others.

SERMON STARTER BACKGROUND

Scripture reading could be read by a person dressed in costume, in a simple set representing a prison cell. This could be done using either an ancient or modern motif.

The name Onesimus means "useful." The name also appears in Colossians 4:9.

According to scholars, slaves were deeded property owned by the men, yet instructed by and commanded by the wives. Slaves became slaves in three ways: (1) being taken in war, (2) being born a slave, and (3) being sold into slavery by creditors or self. Slaves could not receive inheritance.

Under some circumstances slaves could be owned by multiple owners. Or a part of the slave's time could be sold or given to another person to meet an obligation.

The Greco-Roman households (*oikos*) followed a hierarchy of men (master, *kurios*), wives, slave (*doulos*), yet there was an attempt by followers of Christ to be households of mutual submission. There was suspicion they were trying to change the social order; thus, they faced persecution.

Although masculine, *Adelphon*, "brother" in verse 16, is considered inclusive of women as well. Brother-to-sister elevates the status of people to a new relationship. It includes both human and divine relationships. We are "brothered" ones with Christ.

Agapos, verse 16, refers to the "beloved" one—not just loved, but the heir.

Sermon Starter

As alluded to in the Prayers of the People, you could expand on the theme of how people are in bondage to prejudice, expectations, status. Fear of going beyond the self or society-imposed boundaries prevents an individual from changing his or her behavior, let alone working for changes in society.

There was a very definitive role in Paul's day for those who were slaves and those who were masters. Apparently Onesimus stole either money or items from Philemon. Paul is willing to make right the wrong between Philemon and Onesimus by returning the runaway slave, paying the debt, and thus obtaining Onesimus' freedom. In turn, Paul has the expectation that all will be on an equal par as brothers in Christ and that this action will strengthen the life of the Christian community. This was risky expectation, however, for Paul's modeling of Christian households went against the social grain of the Greco-Roman lifestyle. Do radical expectations lead to radical actions?

What can be expected in today's society when one goes against conventional practice? How do we make a decision to stand up for justice rather than accepted practice? Does being a Christian influence our choices? When are the times we speak as individuals, and when do we speak corporately?

SERMON STARTER

A first-person account could be written, selecting one of the named persons in the letter. For example, if Philemon were chosen, he could describe the Onesimus incident and his initial reactions. As a prominent person in the community, surely he was ridiculed for not taking proper care of his slaves. On further reflection, did his initial embarrassment, fear, or anger change when he shared his predicament with the members of the Christian community who met in his house? Was he prepared to receive Paul's letter? Did he take Paul's advice, and if so, how did it make a difference in his relating to Onesimus, Paul, the Christian community, and the local community? If he did not follow Paul's advice, what choice did he make? Did being a follower of Christ impact his decision in any way?

OFFERING MEDITATION

Friends,

Moments ago the children were reminded of those who are "our hearts." How delighted we are to give of our bounty to those who are as close as our own hearts and to causes that pull at our heartstrings.

But the invitation to give goes beyond easy giving and simple solutions. God challenges us to give generously, even sacrificially. Our gifts can offer hope to the unloved and help alleviate the causes of suffering and injustice. This day we particularly remember the ministry of_____
_____(a specific justice ministry of your congregation may be mentioned).

Let us respond by giving our tithes and offerings with hope-filled hearts.

OFFERING PRAYER

Dear God, Heart of our own heart,

Accept our gifts as Paul offered Onesimus back to Philemon, no longer as slave, but as brother and friend, prepared for "all the good we may do for Christ." May we as sisters and brothers in Christ be ever ready to use our talents and our financial resources to make a difference in this world. Amen.

COMMUNION MEDITATION

Through the love they share in Christ, Paul is confident Philemon will receive Onesimus back into his household not as a slave, but as a sibling. With the anticipation of reunion, mended relationships, changed lives, and new possibilities Paul writes: "Refresh my heart in Christ. Prepare for me."

Friends, we too come to this table as Paul did, anxious to be received. Fear not. Here we are welcomed with open arms. By the waters of baptism we are included in the family of faith as heirs of God. There is a place at the table for you, for me. Through the breaking of bread and the pouring of wine the new covenant in Christ is sealed. At this table we are united with God and the saints of all times. The old way is finished and gone; everything becomes fresh and new. Thanks be to God!

Come, all is ready.

BENEDICTION

Rejoice, people of God, within this hour you have been hosted and nourished.

We received sustenance to refresh us on our faith journey.

You leave not alone, but with the life-changing power of God's spirit within you.

We received strength and courage to go out into the world and make a difference.

The grace of the Lord Jesus Christ be with your spirit.

And also with you. Alleluia! Amen! Alleluia!

James

Harvey and May Sweet Lord

CALL TO WORSHIP

God be in our heads and in our thinking.
God be in our hearts and in our loving.
God be in our ears and in our listening.
God be in our hands and in our doing.[1]

OPENING PRAYER

Let the words of our mouths, the meditations of our hearts, and the actions of our limbs be acceptable in your sight, O God, our Strength, and our Redeemer.

PRAYER OF CONFESSION

O God of righteousness,
How far we are from your uprightness.
We see things we know we should do. The days pass,
   and we have not done them. They are on some list,
   now thrown away.
Sick friends we should have called.
Books and magazines we should have read.
Persons with problems to whom we might have
   offered a sympathetic ear.

---

[1]Based on Sarum Primer, 16th century, *Chalice Hymnal* (St. Louis: Chalice Press, 1995), no. 268, amended to reflect emphasis of James.

Children who looked to us for guidance that we did
    not provide.
Forgive us.
There are also things we have done that we know were
    wrong.
Money we should not have spent.
Rich and fast foods we should not have eaten.
Angry words we should not have spoken.
Promises made that we did not keep.
Things that destroy, we have done, and still do!
Forgive and correct us, O God,
For without your help, we may not have the strength to
    change.
Earnestly we pray. Amen.

Words of Assurance

Come now, let us talk this over, says our Lord,
Though your sins are like scarlet, they shall be white as
snow. Though they are red as crimson, they shall be like wool.

Prayers of the People

Members of the congregation are asked to express joys
and concerns. When a "joy" is expressed, the congregation
prays in unison, "Thanks be to you, O God." When a
"concern" is expressed, the congregation prays, "Hear our
prayer, O God."

At the conclusion, the pastor may offer this summary prayer:

We remember the members of our congregation with
    special needs, those that have been mentioned, and
    others we have not named.
We remember the tragedies and disasters in our world
    this week, including those just now reported, and
    also _____.
We remember the poor and those who have been
    pushed to the margins, and we pray on their
    behalf.
We remember those who work in social welfare—
    teachers, counselors, social workers of many kinds—
and ask for them the respect that is their due.

We remember those who risk their lives and their
   possessions to dramatically change our society and
   to make it more just. May their voices be heard.
One day at a time, O Lord, lead us to the Land of
   Promise.
Amen.

CHILDREN'S SERMON

Use this time to talk about doing good works, showing
how God and God's son, Jesus, make us want to practice
doing good works and sharing what we have with others.

SERMON STARTER BACKGROUND

When the book of James was written, the teachings of
Paul were circulating through the scattered Christian
churches in Asia Minor and Europe, either as one or more of
Paul's letters or in some verbal tradition. One main purpose
of James is to enlarge the Christian's understanding of faith
and works. Some were interpreting Paul to say that works
were unimportant and had little if anything to do with our
salvation or our becoming better persons. James responded
that not only was faith essential, but that works were
important as well. "Faith is like that: if good works do not
go with it, it is quite dead" (Jas. 2:17, Jerusalem).

Let us avoid pitting James against Paul as if to say that if
one is right, the other must be wrong. Our Christian heritage
tells us that we can learn from each of them. The fact that the
writings of both Paul and James are in our scriptures means
that they impressed our forebears in the church as being
valuable resources for those who want to live a Christian life.

Martin Luther called James "The Straw Gospel." We
suggest "The Practical Gospel."

Theme: In living out our faith, it is important to strive for
correct behavior patterns, also known as "good works." We
need to eliminate bad habits and establish and keep good ones.

SERMON STARTER: WHEN GOOD PEOPLE HAVE BAD HABITS

Today it is natural to talk about "works" in the familiar
terms of social science. Good works = "good behavior." We

could interpret "muscles" as a poetic contrast to the image of "heart." Muscles would be a metaphor for actions. Practiced Christian muscles could be equivalent to good habits. Good habits can become so normal to us that we seldom think about them—we just do them. As an athlete's muscles developed with careful practice do, they automatically put the basketball through the hoop.

Our unseen, inward faith is important, but people will pass judgments on us based on our actions. We can think of good behavior as faith in action, faith in motion, embodied faith, incarnate faith, one that makes use of our heart and our muscles.

One simple way to say this: "I know they talk the talk, but do they walk the walk?" Puzzle about this: Why did I come to church this morning? Because I believe I should? Yes, but I believe in many things and do only some of them. Then why did I? Because I regularly come to church! Yes, it may be in my pattern of behavior, a good habit. I may even be unaware of choosing to come or not to come. I developed the habit years ago, and now my faith is working through my muscles.

Faith in our hearts leads to faith in our muscles. And maybe faith in our muscles could lead to faith in our hearts. Good habits lead us to church each Sunday, and in church our faith may be strengthened.

One of the things we can learn even today from our Jewish cousins-in-faith is that rules and regulations can teach us good habits, and good habits can make life much better for all concerned. This person has old parents in a nursing home. He thinks they are the greatest parents in the world, but in fact, as busy as his life is, he seldom sees them, even though they are only fifteen minutes away. Another person rarely thinks about her parents, but by established habits visits them once a week, half an hour away. Which is better: mind righteousness or muscle righteousness? Or both? Our nonworshiping neighbors make judgments about the church. They see that in our worship we have beautiful things to say, but in our behavior both in and out of the church, we are pretty much like other people. They do not want words; they want actions. In forming the Disciples Justice Action Network, younger members of our group tended to insist that we have the word *Action* in our title and that we have it in our life together as well. What was our network doing about justice? I think James would applaud these young adults.

James (1:25) talks about "the perfect law of freedom." It may seem strange to link a law that proscribes behavior with freedom. Here is at least part of what James is trying to say. Good moral laws give us freedom by planting righteousness in our behavior patterns and freeing us from the frozenness of having to decide every action as a brand new moral choice.

An army private was given KP duty. He had to sort fifty pounds of potatoes into three baskets. The large ones went here, the middle-sized there, and the small ones in yet another basket. The corporal came back a couple of hours later, and the private was a mess, his hair awry and his eyes wild. The corporal looked at the private, who had sorted less than ten pounds! There he was tearing his hair and muttering: "Decisions, Decisions, Decisions!" The law of freedom lets you establish good habits, freeing you from having to decide everything anew.

You have faith? Then get those habits right. It frees you from a lot of wear and tear, and it helps your faith to practice itself. Some good habits, according to James, are:

Be a good listener.

Control your tongue, especially when angry.

Make accurate judgments of yourself, "looking in a mirror and remembering."

Help those in need, such as "orphans and widows."

Keep yourself uncontaminated by the world.

Final Appeal: I suggest that most sermons should close with an appeal for personal change in behavior. You might want to appeal to worshipers to break a bad habit and begin a new good one.

SERMON STARTER

The Christian faith envisions a world in which there will no longer be rich and poor, but the gifts of God will be equally divided. You and I, because of our faith, ought to work for such a world.

Please use the Jerusalem Bible with its references: James 1:9–11; 2:1–13—"riches last no longer than the flower in the grass" (1:10), "it was those who are poor according to the world that God chose, to be rich in faith and to be heirs to the kingdom which he promised to those who love him" (2:5).

Related Scripture: "How happy (Blessed) are you who are poor: yours is the kingdom of God" (Lk. 6:20b, Jerusalem).

Biblical Background: See Zephaniah 2:3 "the humble of the earth" and the note (e) in the Jerusalem Bible on the "humble," "poor," and *anawim*." See also 1 Samuel 2:7–8; Psalm 72:4, and Luke 1:52. See also Matthew 5:3, note (c) in the Jerusalem Bible.

Sermon Title: "Some Get Rich, Some Get Poor" or "Greed and Glory."

Sermon Ideas: There are two conflicting themes in our lives as North American Christians. It appears America's theme is open competition. Here it is possible for the poor to become rich and the rich to become poor. From our American perspective, it is best to be rich, and duty is laid on us to try. Parents are disappointed if their children don't "make good money." This view seems to encourage greed.

Are you familiar with this form of the Golden Rule— "The one who has the gold rules!"? Our biblical heritage suggests a different view. The community that God promises is a turnaround world in which the poor will be elevated and the rich humbled. All will be brothers and sisters around one banquet table.

A careful examination of our scripture opens a meaning that a quick glance misses. We do not have much detail about the early churches other than the Jerusalem congregation and certain others to whom Paul wrote. We know that in Jerusalem there was an effort to share and share alike. People were acting in anticipation of the new age that was coming. "The whole group of believers was united, heart and soul; no one claimed for his own use anything that he had, as everything they owned was held in common" (Acts 4:32, Jerusalem).

And from our scripture today it sounds as if Jerusalem may not have been the only church that practiced this. James (1:9) suggests the anticipated situation in the world to come may be already practiced in several churches. "It is right for the poor brother to be proud of his high rank" suggests that a way has been found to elevate "the poor brother" in the life of the church. Does "and the rich one to be thankful that he has been humbled" mean that the churches had a "humbling" practice in which the rich divested themselves on behalf of the church community? Sounds like it. If so, the practice did not long continue. We know that the church later in its history imitated the greed it found around itself, envied the rich, and hastened to become rich.

In North American society, the gulf between rich and poor grows wider each day. And we know that almost all North Americans can be counted as rich compared to incomes of Third World persons. Never in history have nations been as wealthy as our North American ones are today. You and I are beneficiaries of the wealth, reaping its advantages.

Even in the world we know, which encourages competition and greed, we feel badly that there are poor among us. Partly out of guilt and partly by conviction we attempt to provide a safety net for the poor. However, this is not sharing the wealth in the biblical sense; it is just making poverty more tolerable.

Two social requirements in the society of the United States help reduce the gulf between rich and poor: the graduated income tax, and estate taxes. We require high-income persons to give up a greater share of their income to serve the general needs of our nation. And we give financial assistance through the income tax system to the poor. Both the graduated income tax and the inheritance tax would need to be substantially increased if we were to have an egalitarian society. Unfortunately, the political winds are blowing against that possibility for both. Their impact may be reduced. The gulf may grow wider.

How do we practice economic justice in the church? in society? How do we avoid class distinctions that cause differences in the way our members are treated? How do we live today as if the new and just world is about to arrive? How can we in the church live out a witness against greed and in favor of egalitarianism? Shall we take vows of poverty and enter a monastery, as some Christians have done through the ages? Is there a possibility of a disciplined witness in the midst of life in the world?

Here are examples to think about: A pacifist minister kept his salary so low that he never had to pay taxes and thus avoided supporting the American military. A vegetarian decided that eating at the top of the food chain is an inexcusable habit of the rich. One concerned about pollution owns no car and uses public transportation. A couple lived at a subsistence level all their lives and gave all above this to overseas missions. A man decided he did not need a closet full of clothes and reduced them to three outfits. (In many parts of the world, people have only one public outfit, which they wash and iron daily.)

Appeal to Action: Will you develop a new habit that you choose as a way to keep your own life from greed? Will you live, even in a symbolic way, a life of poverty?

Offering Meditation

The mystery of life is in God's hands. Will there be food for tomorrow? In trust we bring the tithes of all we get, and offerings as well.

Offering Prayer

Take our moneys, O God. Make them holy and effective. May the day of full sharing draw near. Amen.

Communion Meditation

On the first day of every week, we gather and celebrate the remarkable love Jesus has for us.

Knowing all our weaknesses, Jesus loved us in advance and left us with a promise.

Each first day speaks of that future day, when there shall be neither slave nor free, Jew nor Gentile, gay nor straight, rich nor poor,

For there shall be one family, with Jesus in our midst, and we shall share and share alike.
Come and eat with us this meal.
(The peace is passed; communion is celebrated.)

BENEDICTION

The Lord bless you and keep you,
The Lord make his face to shine upon you and be gracious unto you.
The Lord lift up the light of her countenance upon you and give you peace. Amen.

Hymn and Anthem Suggestions

Judith Ann Brown

HYMN SUGGESSTIONS

Code for *Use* column: O=opening, P=prayer, S=sermon,
C=communion, E=ending

Hymnals: *Chalice Hymnal, The United Methodist Hymnal, The
Presbyterian Hymnal, The New Century Hymnal* (United Church
of Christ).

AT means alternate title.

Scripture and Hymn Title	Use	Chal	UMH	Pres	UCC
Genesis 18:1–15					
The God of Abraham Praise	O,E	24	116	488	24
God of Abraham and Sarah	O,E	-	-	-	20
Kum ba Yah	P	590	494	338	-
O (Our) God, Our Help in Ages Past	S,E	67	117	210	25
God of Our Life	S,E	713	-	275	366
Great Is Thy Faithfulness	O,S	86	140	276	423
There's a Wideness in God's Mercy	P,S,E	73	121	298	23
O God Whose Steadfast Love (st.2)	S	-	-	-	426
Here at Thy Table, Lord	C	384	-	-	-
O God, Unseen Yet Ever Near	C	399	-	-	-
Exodus 5:1—6:1					
God of Many Names	O	13	105	-	-
Immortal, Invisible, God Only Wise	O	66	103	263	1
Precious Lord, Take My Hand	P,C	628	474	404	472

Scripture and Hymn Title	Use	Chal	UMH	Pres	UCC
If You Will Trust in God to Guide You	P,S,E	565	142 (AT)	282	410
Go Down, Moses	S,E	663	448	334	572
Come, You Disconsolate	P,C	502	510	-	-
We Shall Overcome	P,S,E	630	533	-	570
Lift Every Voice	S,E	631	519	563	593
Lead On, O Cloud of Presence	S,E	633	-	-	-
Let My People Seek Their Freedom	S,E	-	586	-	-
I Hunger and I Thirst	C	409	-	-	-
All Who Hunger, Gather Gladly	C	419	-	-	-

2 Kings 4:1–37

I'll Praise My Maker	O	20	60	253	-
Sing Praise to God	O	6	126	483	6
There Is a Balm in Gilead	P	501	375	394	553
Be Still, My Soul	P,S	566	534	-	488
God Hath Spoken by the Prophets	S,E	-	108	-	-
How Firm a Foundation	S,E	618	529	361	407
The Voice of God Is Calling	S,E	666	436	-	-
We've Come This Far by Faith	E	533	-	-	-
For the Bread	C	411	614,615	508,509	-
We Place upon Your Table	C	417	-	-	-

Jeremiah 18:1–11

Great Is Thy Faithfulness	O	86	140	-	423
Come, Thou Fount of Every Blessing	O	16	400	356	459
All My Hope Is Firmly Grounded	O	88(AT)	132	-	-
Have Thine Own Way, Lord	P	588	382	-	-
Spirit of the Living God	P	259	393	322	283
Yo Quiero Ser (I Want to Be)	P	520	-	-	-
Trust and Obey	S,E	556	467	-	-
O God of Earth and Altar	S,E	724	-	291	582
God of Grace and God of Glory	S,E	464	577	420	436
When Our Confidence Is Shaken	S,E	534	505	-	-
These I Lay Down	C	391	-	-	-
Bread of the World, in Mercy Broken	C	387	624	502	346

Micah 4:1–6

O for a Thousand Tongues to Sing	O	5	57	466	42
God of the Sparrow	O	70	122	272	32
O Day of God, Draw Nigh (Near)	P,S	700	730	452	611
Lead Me, Guide Me	P	583	-	-	-
Dear Lord, and Father of Mankind (Dear God, Embracing Humankind)	P	594	358	345	502
O for a World (Azmon)	S,E	683	-	386	575
O God of Every Nation	S,E	680	435	289	-
Down by the Riverside	S,E	673	-	-	-
Today We All Are Called to Be Disciples	S,E	-	-	434	-
O Day of Peace That Dimly Shines	P,S,E	711	729	450	-
I Come with Joy	C	420	617	507	349
All Who Hunger, Gather Gladly	C	419	-	-	-

Scripture and Hymn Title	Use	Chal	UMH	Pres	UCC
Matthew 4:23—5:16					
Lift High the Cross	O	108	159	371	198
A Mighty Fortress	O	65	110	260	439,440
In Suff'ring Love	P	212	-	-	-
I Want Jesus to Walk (Go) With Me	P	627	521	363	490
Near to the Heart of God	P,C	581	472	527	-
How Firm a Foundation	S,E	618	529	361	407
Blessed Are the Poor in Spirit	S,E	-	-	-	180
You Are Salt for the Earth	S,E	-	-	-	181
I Want to Walk As a Child of the Light	S,E	-	206	-	-
Sois la Semilla (You Are the Seed)	E	478	583	-	528
Become to Us the Living Bread	C	423	630	500	-
Lo, I Am with You	C	430	-	-	-
Matthew 20:20–28					
You (Ye) Servants of God	O	110	181	477	305
When Morning Gilds the Skies	O	100	185	487	86
Jesus Calls Us	P,S	337	398	-	171,172
O Master, Let Me Walk with Thee	P,S	602	430	357	-
Tu Has Venido a la Orilla	P,S	342	344	377	173
(Lord, You Have Come to the Lakeshore)					
Called as Partners to Christ's Service	S,E	453	-	343	495
I Am Thine (Yours), O Lord	S,E	601	419	-	455
Sister, (Won't You) Let Me	S,E	490	-	-	539
Be Your Servant					
Let Us Talents and Tongues Employ	C	422	-	514	347
Draw Us in the Spirit's Tether	C	392	632	504	337
Matthew 22:34–40					
Christ Is Made the Sure Foundation	O	275	559	416,417	400
Christians, We Have Met to Worship	O	277	-	-	-
The God of Abraham Praise	O	24	116	488	24
Spirit of God, Descend upon My Heart	P	265	500	326	290
Spirit of the Living God	P	259	393	322	283
There's a Spirit in the Air	S,E	257	192	433	294
If You Will Trust in God to Guide You	S,E	565	142(AT)	282	410
Jesus a New Commandment	S,E	-	-	-	389
Has Given Us (Un mandamiento nuevo)					
Lord God, Your Love Has Called Us Here	S,E	-	579	-	-
Lord, Make Me (Us) More Holy	P,E	-	-	536	75
Eat This Bread	C	414	628	-	-
These I Lay Down	C	391	-	-	-
Matthew 25:31–46					
Come, Thou (Now) Almighty King (God)	O	27	61	139	275
God Is Here	O	280	660	461	70
The Gift of Love (Though I May Speak)	P	526	408	335	-
Open My Eyes, That I May See	P	586	454	324	-
like a Child	S,E	133	-	-	-
Alleluia! Hear God's Story	S,E	330	-	-	-

Scripture and Hymn Title	Use	Chal	UMH	Pres	UCC
The Church of Christ in Every Age	S,E	475	589	421	306
Pues Si Vivimos (When We Are Living)	S,E	536	356	400	-
Christian Women, Christian Men	S,E	-	-	348	-
Una Espiga (Sheaves of Summer)	C	396	637	518	338
An Upper Room Did Our Lord Prepare	C	385	-	94	-

Luke 1:39–56

My Soul Gives Glory to My God	O,S	130	198	600	119
Tell Out, My Soul	O,S	-	200	-	-
Hail to the Lord's Anointed	O	140	203	-	104(AT)
Come, Thou (O) Long-expected Jesus	O,S	125	196	1,2	122
Christians All, Your Lord Is Coming	O,E,C	136	-	-	-
Give Thanks	P	528	-	-	-
Creator of the Stars	P	127	692	4	111(AT)
All Earth Is Waiting	S,E	139	210	-	121
O for a World	P,S,E	683	-	386	575
I Am the Light of the World	S,E	469	-	-	584
Become to Us the Living Bread	C	423	630	500	-
Now the Silence	C	415	619	-	-

Luke 4:16–30

Jesus Shall Reign	O	95	157	423	300
Blessed Be the God of Israel	O	135	209	-	-
I'll Praise My Maker	O	20	60	253	-
Open My Eyes, That I May See	P	586	454	324	-
Who Would Ever Have Believed It?	P	213	-	-	-
Spirit of Faith, Come Down	P	-	332	-	-
O Young and Fearless Prophet	S,E	669	444	-	-
Live into Hope	S,E	-	-	332	-
Arise, Your Light Is Come	S,E	-	-	-	164
Help Us Accept Each Other	S,E	487	560	358	388
We Come as Guests Invited	C	386	-	517	-
You Satisfy the Hungry Heart	C	429	629	521	-

Luke 10:25–37

Come, Christians, Join to Sing	O	90	158	150	-
All Hail the Power of Jesus' Name	O	91,92	154,155	142,143	304
Jesus Calls Us	P	337	398	-	171,172
Where Charity and Love Prevail	P	-	549	-	396
Jesu, Jesu	S,C,E	600	432	367	498
There's a Spirit in the Air	S,E	257	192	433	294
Alleluia! Hear God's Story	S,E	330	-	-	-
We Are Your People	S,E	-	-	436	-
They Asked "Who's My Neighbor?"	S,E	-	-	-	541
Lord, Whose Love Through Humble Service	S,E	461	581	427	-
One Bread, One Body	C	393	620	-	-
Let Us Break Bread Together	C	425	618	513	330

Scripture and Hymn Title	Use	Chal	UMH	Pres	UCC
Luke 16:19–31					
Praise, My Soul, the God of Heaven	O	23	66	478,479	273(AT)
Love Divine, All Loves Excelling	O,S,E	517	384	376	43
Jesus, Remember Me	P	569	488	599	-
Jesus, Lover of My Soul	P	542	479	303	546
Through All the World a Hungry Christ	P,S	-	-	-	587
Cuando el Pobre (When the Poor Ones)	S,E	662	434	407	-
Your Love, O God	S,E	71	120	-	-
Where Cross the Crowded Ways of Life	S,E	665	427	408	543
We Are Called to Follow Jesus	S,E	465	-	-	-
Lord, Whose Love Through Humble Service	S,E	461	581	427	-
For the Bread, Which You Have Broken	C	411	614,615	508,509	-
Here, O My Lord, I See Thee Face to Face	C	416	623	520	336
Philemon					
Rejoice, You Pure in Heart	O	15	160,161	145,146	55,71
Come, Be Glad!	O	329	-	-	-
Gather Us In	O	284	-	-	-
Amazing Grace	P	546	378	280	547,548
There's a Wideness in God's Mercy	P	73	121	298	23
Lord, Make Us Servants of Your Peace	P	-	-	374	-
Called as Partners in Christ's Service	S,E	453	-	343	-
Sister, (Won't You) Let Me Be Your Servant	S,E	490	-	-	539
Help Us Accept Each Other	S,E	487	560	358	388
In Christ There Is No East or West	S,E	687	548	439,440	394,395
One Bread, One Body	C	393	620	-	-
Una Espiga (Sheaves of Summer)	C	396	637	518	338
James					
Sing Praise to God	O	6	126	483	6
Praise, My Soul, the God of Heaven	O	23	66	478,479	273(AT)
Lord, I Want to Be a Christian	P	589	402	372	454
Come Down (Forth), O Love Divine	P	582	475	313	289
Now It Is Evening	S,E	471	-	-	-
Pues Si Vivimos (When We Are Living)	S,E	536	356	400	-
The Church of Christ in Every Age	S,E	475	589	421	306
When the Church of Jesus	S,E	470	592	-	-
Where Cross the Crowded Ways of Life	S,E	665	427	408	543
As a Chalice Cast of Gold	C,S,E	287	-	336	-
I Come with Joy	C	420	617	507	349
Come, Share the Lord	C	408	-	-	-

Anthem Suggestions

In many instances a hymn or anthem is appropriate for more than one lesson. Check with other lessons having similar themes. Hymns are named no more than two times. Anthems are not repeated, although another setting of the same tune is named twice.

Augsburg has recently started using ISBN numbers to identify anthems. Those numbers are in parentheses at the end of each listing.

Genesis 18:1–15

Great Is Thy Faithfulness
Runyan/Schrader
Hope CH 672 SAB; C5081 SATB

Day by Day
Mark Hayes
Augsburg Fortress 11-10962 SATB
(0-8006-5834-5)

If You Will Trust the Lord to Guide You
Kenneth Kosche
Morning Star MSM-50-9108 SAB

Exodus 5:1—6:1

Precious Lord, Take My Hand
Dorsey/Schrader
Hope GC 968 SATB; GC988 SAB

Saints Bound for Heaven
Parker and Shaw
Warner Bros. LG00911 SATB

The Power of Your Name
Dana Mengel
Abingdon 095581 SAB

2 Kings 4:1–37

The Lord Be Near Us
Hal Hopson
Morning Star MSM-50-7038 SATB

Hymn of Promise
Natalie Sleeth
Hope A 580 2 pt; A686 SATB

Balm in Gilead
Mark Shepperd
Augsburg 11-10923 SATB (0-8006-5791-8)

Jeremiah 18:1–11

Called by the Spirit
John Horman
Choristers Guild CGA734 Unison, 2 pt.

Have Your Own Way, Lord
Dana Mengel
Abingdon 02712-8 SATB

Offertory
John Ness Beck
Beckenhorst BP1280 SATB

Micah 4:1–6

The Promise of Peace
K. Lee Scott
Morning Star MSM-50 8903 SATB

Peace Is Our Prayer
Larry Shackley
Beckenhorst BP1539 SATB

Song of Hope
Tom Mitchell
Choristers Guild
CGA638 Unison plus descants

Matthew 4:23—5:16

Blessed Are You
Craig Courtney
Beckenhorst BP1538 SATB

Blest Are They
David Haas
GIA G-2958 Unison, 2pt, SAB

I Want to Walk as a Child of the Light
Paul Manz
Morning Star MSM-60-9019 SATB

Matthew 20:20–28

I Want to Walk as a Child of the Light
Richard Erickson
Augsburg 11-10957 SATB (0-8006-5839-6)

Lord of Lords, Adored by Angels
Paul Bouman
Morning Star MSM-50-9025 SATB

Take Up Your Cross
Hal Hopson
Augsburg 11-10570 2 pt. mixed
(0-8006-5450-1)

Matthew 22:34–40

Lord, I Want to Be a Christian
Jewel Thompson
Morning Star MSM-50-9038 SATB

Our God Is Love
Nancy DeVries
Abingdon 073901—2 Pt.

Your Spirit, God, Moves Us to Pray
John Horman
Abingdon 071240 SATB

Matthew 25:31–46

Catch the Vision! Share the Glory!
Carl Schalk
Morning Star MSM-50-6006 SATB

Pues Si Vivimos (When We Are Living)
Hal Hopson
Augsburg 11-10966 SATB
(0-8006-5830-2)

So Much We Have
John Horman
Abingdon 087686 Unison

The Lord Will Guide
Robert Powell
Augsburg 11-10599 SATB (0-8006-5475-7)

Luke 1:39–56

Canticle of the Turning
Rory Cooney
GIA G-3407 SAT

My Soul Gives Glory to the Lord
Carl Schalk
Morning Star MSM-50-1058 SATB

Luke 1:39–56 (continued)

A New Magnificat
Carolyn Jennings
Augsburg 11-10479 SATB (0-8006-5255-X)

Tell Out, My Soul
K. Lee Scott
Concordia 98-3096 SATB

Luke 4:16–30

I Will Greatly Rejoice in the Lord
Philip Young
Concordia 98-3093 Unison

This Is God's Beloved Son
John Horman
Abingdon 072247 SAB

With the Help of the Spirit of the Lord
Jayne Cool
Choristers Guild CGA-508 Unison, 2 pt

Luke 10:25–37

Lord, Let Us Listen
Robert Hobby
Augsburg 11-11062 Unison, 2 pt.
(0-8006-5923-6)

Prayer for Today
Margaret Tucker
Choristers Guild CGA 358 Unison;
CGA855 SATB

Walk in Light
Bob Burroughs
Abingdon 07165-8 SATB

Luke 16:19–31

Pues Si Vivimos (While We Are Living)
Alice Parker
Hal Leonard 08596533 SATB

Hunger Cries
John Horman
Sacred Music Press 10/1517S SATB

I Want Jesus to Walk with Me
Hal Hopson
Choristers Guild CGA701 2 pt

Treasure
Michael Graham
Concordia 98-3541 SATB

Philemon

Build New Bridges
Wayne Wold
Augsburg 11-10879 Unison, 2 pt.
(0-8006-5743-8)

Make Me a Channel of Your Peace
Temple/Holstein
Hope A733 SATB; 2 pt. mixed A722

Servants of Peace
K. Lee Scott
Selah 425-822 SATB

Trust and Obey
Dana Mengel
Abingdon 073308 SATB

James

Come, Labor On
John Ferguson
Morning Star MSM-50-6502 SATB

Do All the Good You Can
Townley/Wiens
Abingdon 071747 SAT

Prayer for Partnership
Tom Mitchell
Choristers Guild CGA539 SAB or SATB

Small Deeds
John Horman
Choristers Guild CGA562 Unison/2 pt.

BIBLE QUEST TEXTS

This book of worship resources may be used on its own, but it also coordinates with the BIBLE QUEST curriculum for congregational education. The justice and liberation theme for BIBLE QUEST year 3 contains fifteen Bookmark Stories based on the scriptures listed below:

Genesis 18:1–15

Exodus 2:1–12; 12—14

2 Kings 4:1–37

Micah 4:1–8

Luke 1:39–56

Luke 4:16–30

Luke 10:25–37

Luke 16:19–31

Matthew 20:20–28

Matthew 22:34–40

Matthew 25:31–46

Philemon

Jeremiah 18:1–6

Matthew 4:23—5:16

James 1:22—2:26